Rock Bottom at the Renaissance

*An Emo Kid's Journey Through
Falling In and Out of Love
In and With New York City*

by Mike Henneberger

Berger Media | New York

Join The Berger Joint Email List
And Preview Mike's Next Book For Free
As It Comes Together.

Sign Up At
RockBottomBook.com

Follow The Author:

Instagram: @MikeyLeeRock
Twitter: @MikeyLeeRock
Facebook.com/MikeyLeeRock

Follow A Berger Joint For Rock Bottom
Video Content, and Get More Cool Sh*t
To Read, See, and Watch:

Instagram: @aBergerJoint
Twitter: @aBergerJoint
Facebook.com/aBergerJoint
YouTube.com/aBergerJoint

And For Interviews About The Book
and Audiobook Chapters Subscribe To
A Berger Joint Podcast.

HEAR EVERY SONG IN THE BOOK ON THE ROCK BOTTOM PLAYLIST

Scan With Your Phone For Spotify:

Scan With Your Phone For Apple Music:

Rock Bottom at the Renaissance

*An Emo Kid's Journey Through
Falling In and Out of Love
In and With New York City*

For any questions about the book or the author, or for media or speaking engagement requests contact RockBottomBook@aBergerJoint.com.

A Berger Joint Published in the United States by Berger Media LLC, New York

Library of Congress Control Number: 2019910292
Library of Congress Cataloging-In-Publication Data
Names: Henneberger, Mike, author.
Title: Rock Bottom at the Renaissance: An Emo Kid's Journey Through Falling In and Out of Love In and With New York City / Mike Henneberger.

Identifiers: ISBN 978-1-7333513-5-5 (paperback)
ISBN 978-1-7333513-1-7 (ebook)
ISBN 978-1-7333512-3-1 (audiobook)

Subjects: mental health, memoir, biography, music

If you or someone you know is struggling with depression, anxiety, addiction, or even just occasional shitty feelings or thoughts you think no one else struggles with, these folks are here to help. The author and publisher are not affiliated with these organization, other than Zero Platoon, nor have these organizations endorsed this book. Hopefully they will though.

National Suicide Prevention Lifeline 1-800-273-8255

Veterans Crisis Line 1-800-273-8255 (Press 1)
or chat online at www.VeteransCrisisLine.net

The Trevor Project 866-488-7386
or chat online at www.TheTrevorProject.org
Crisis intervention and suicide prevention services to young people in the LGBTQ community.

Crisis Text Line: Text HOME to 741741
Free, 24/7 Crisis Support in the US

National Drug Helpline 1-844-289-0879

To Write Love on Her Arms www.twloha.com

Hope For The Day www.hftd.org

Zero Platoon www.ZeroPlatoon.com
Fighting For Military Mental Health

*To The Girl, and to all the bands that kept me alive
long enough to find her.*

Listen.

If anything, I am a music nerd. I'm not sure if I'd ever call myself a musician. In fact, it is because of my music nerdiness that I would never call myself a musician. I was a lead singer in two bands during a time span of seven years, toured the country a few times, and even played a coliseum in front of 10-15,000 people—twice. While I always wrote my own lyrics, I never wrote music. I can play guitar—kinda. But it's been over a decade since the first time I picked one up, and I'm still not quite confident enough to perform solo in front of anyone except for girls I've really liked. And even then it requires a good amount of alcohol and a bigger amount of emotional investment. So I'll never call myself a musician, but I do call myself a writer.

When I was younger, I didn't quite understand what led me to playing music or writing lyrics. As I've gotten older and examined my experiences, certain puzzle pieces have come together and begun to form a picture that makes more and more sense with every jig-sawed piece. I remember my dad playing records all the time when I was a kid. My parents divorced when I was seven or eight, and when my brother and I would spend weeks at a time with dad during the summers, I remember waking up to vinyl records spinning in the morning—The Cure, Bruce Springsteen, Prince, and old country like Conway Twitty and Johnny Cash and Patsy Cline. I was blessed with an upbringing in Texas, and a dad with Oklahoma roots who found some musical enlightenment in the culture collision that 20+ years of Navy service give you. Back then I didn't know how much of an effect that would have on me, but today I know that's when it all began. I remember listening to those songs closely and letting their meaning really affect me. Maybe an eight-year-old mind can't exactly decipher "Just Like Heaven," but I remember crying in the front seat of my dad's car while Conway Twitty's "That's My Job" played as he was driving me from Oklahoma to south Texas to return me to my mom's full-custody after one of those summer trips. When you're a kid, your parents aren't people; they're just mom and dad. My dad was still trying to figure his life out back then, but to me he was just a dad who wasn't close enough to his kids. Because he took that time, he has since figured himself out. It's been over twenty years, and Mom's still behind the curve. I always wondered if those songs helped him get through the lonely times when his kids were a thousand miles away, or when another girlfriend (or in some cases, another wife) didn't work out.

My subconscious must have put my dad's connection to music together back then, because I began to see life through music. My dad always had the latest in stereo equipment, and he always took really good care of his records. I saw that music was important to him, and I guess something made me want to know why. For years, I have been the same way with my music. I get paid to write about it because I write about it with a passion that isn't matched by anything else—not even women. I'm maybe five years younger than my dad was when he and my mother divorced. Had I gotten married as young as he had, I definitely wouldn't have lasted as long. Dad's on wife number four now, and it looks like he finally got it right. I don't have kids to miss, but there are ex-girlfriends whom I loved, and songs that make me think of them. Music not only gets me through those lonely times, those depressing times, but also the good moments. It was loneliness in high school that kick-started my writing. I didn't know it was what I would be doing for the next decade-and-a-half. I started writing lyrics for my band. And this brings me to my first point: My lyrics *sucked* at first. But after writing songs for years, they got better. I don't expect this book to be gold, but no one would see it if I wasn't proud of it. Maybe in ten years, I will say that my first book sucked. That just means I will be that much better then.

I'm telling you about my history and future and life of music because you should know your author before you read his work. For years I have written songs, and I have written comedy for myself and funnier friends to perform. Although, this book probably won't be very funny. I've talked with my friends about a certain evolution many comedians go through. First they joke about being lonely and never getting laid. Then, if they're lucky enough to rise in popularity and actually meet a woman who really does want a sense of humor, they'll get married. Then they have material about being married and never getting laid. Then, because a lot of comics are tortured men who are filled with demons, they get divorced and joke about being divorced and bitter (and never getting laid). The same is also true for records. No one wants to hear a great songwriter when they're in a happy relationship. I think it's safe to say that a lot of musicians (or the ones worth listening to) pick up a pen or an instrument because they were lonely and weren't getting laid. But an album does not necessarily tell a story from beginning to end; rather, it tells what state of mind that songwriter was in. A comic's set doesn't tell a story from first joke to last; a good comic maintains a steady voice throughout the set, so you feel like you know the performer. Or, so the performer at least makes you feel like you know the persona that they want you to know.

I remember one of my former bosses and I were talking about The Gaslight Anthem one day. We were both fans of the band, and he offered me his tickets to their show that night. He was a few years older than me, but had recently hit that point when life and/or your body catches up to you and you just can't go to every show on a school night like you used to. I was a few years younger than him, and my professional life kicked off a little later than most. So, I was at that point when you still want to go to all the shows, but you're in an entry level position and not making enough money to buy all the tickets. He was a great boss, and I'd like to think it's because I was a great employee that, on more than one occasion, this worked out in my favor. And to his credit, and in his defense, it was usually when certain bands played multiple nights in the New York City area and the young punk inside of him would convince him to buy tickets to every night. It's how I discovered Quicksand, who were as good as he told me they'd be. It's how I got to see Bad Religion at Terminal 5. And it's how I saw The Gaslight Anthem for the first time. Also at Terminal 5.

We got to talking about our appreciation for the band, and he made a joke about how, in their songs, they seem to be listening to the radio a lot. "Nobody listens to the radio anymore," he said. And that's when I realized that, for some reason, we demand that musicians, more than any other artists, be authentic. If we step away from an artist, after a song ends, give it some distance, we might be able to accept that there's a bit of persona there. But when we're listening to a song, something in our minds makes us feel and think that this person singing to us is giving it to us, as Bryan Adams would say, "straight from the heart." Shit, was that even real?

"It's the band's persona," I told him.

When we watch a movie, we know those characters aren't who the actors are in real life. Why do we demand different from our musicians? Is an artist's painting or sculpture a direct reflection of their personality? Yet, Taylor Swift is painted as this vindictive monster who uses relationships for song ideas, when maybe she's just a storyteller who knows that some people need to hear these stories so they feel like someone else gets them. Are Brian Fallon and company dragging main in a '59 Impala convertible, rocking The Coasters, hair slicked back, racing an "Old White Lincoln" under the hot New Jersey summer sun? I don't know. Maybe. Or maybe they're just painting this picture, not of a specific time, but of a state of mind. And even if that picture never existed, isn't that the point? Putting that state of mind into a song, on a canvas, on these white pages, makes it exist. It makes us feel like it could exist––for better or worse. If it's for better, then maybe it inspires us to strive for it. If it's for worse, like some of the stories in this book—real or not—then hopefully it has the same effect, and helps us to avoid mistakes that would be too easy to make, and motivates us to move further away from the ones we've already made. Does it matter whether or not certain things happened the way a writer (an "artist") remembers, or imagines, or wishes they had, or hopes they will, or knows they could've had they been unluckier or luckier? No matter what, the artist's state of mind when creating their art was true, and the state of mind you're left with after consuming the art is as true as it gets, no?

So, forgive me, I am not a seasoned author. I am a writer of jokes, songs, and critical essays. If you read all of those things—like listening to most albums—you will not find closure in the end. My only goal was to write something, get it on paper, and get it out to people. I wanted my "first effort" to exist, so I can move on to the next. I'm not making preemptive excuses. I'm a pretty proud writer. I don't put something out if I think it's shit. So...what you hold in your hands now is something I am proud of. Some great writers had shitty first works. Some authors with brilliant first works could never live up to that debut—Fitzgerald, Harper Lee, Salinger. I'd like to find myself somewhere in the middle and give myself room to grow. Maybe one day I'll be a better writer and I'll write books with beginnings, middles, and ends. Maybe this book will have those things, and I'll achieve that goal. Maybe I'll make people believe in something. I'm not sure if that's even what I want. I do know that I want to make people feel something. I had the same goal when I wrote songs, and I had the same goal when I got on stage and told jokes. And in that goal, I feel confident in this work.

I'm a music nerd. I think in songs. Not like a musical in my head, but I think in song lyrics. Some people might think to themselves, "the Bible says this about this situation," or "that book I read says this," or maybe in principles of science, philosophy, or psychology. I think in song lyrics and live in an album world. Pop this one on the player and see what the writer was feeling. The last song might have nothing to do with the first song. One or two songs may be good enough to be a single, but they're not all supposed to be. Who knows where I will be in life when it's time to write the next one, but I didn't hold anything back in writing this one. So, in reading it, you will know exactly where I was when I wrote it. Figuratively. The title is all you need to know where I was literally.

"23" – Jimmy Eat World

This is stupid. I call myself a writer. I once had a discussion with this guy who was, at the time, my best friend. This guy came up with a good idea for a book, or at least an idea for a book. He started working on it and one day asked me, "Does this mean I'm an author?" I said no. Authors are published. Writers are bitter.

I call myself a writer but I don't write. It's not because I can't. I'm actually pretty damn good at it. That is to say, I really don't give a shit what anyone else thinks. My writing is incredibly scrutinized…by me. I go over and over it, I Google grammar questions, I check spellings of words I'm sure of, and I fall down black holes of research just to make whatever 80's pop culture reference perfectly accurate. If a reader doesn't like it, well, fuck them. I'm the worst kind of writer: one who writes for himself. Hello, unstable future! As long as I think it's good, that's all that matters to me. That's not what I meant by "this is stupid." If I thought that writing this book was stupid, I would do things differently. For instance, I'm in a hotel room for a weekend, and the first things I packed were some Ambien (for insomnia), Adderall (for A.D.D.), Xanax (for anxiety), cigarettes (for boredom) and a bottle of Johnnie Walker (for fun). Clothes and personal hygiene essentials were thrown on top of the necessities. Stupid? Possibly. If I thought so, I'd change my methods. Here's *a* stupid thing, not *the* stupid thing: I don't subscribe to the philosophy that great writers must abuse drugs and/or alcohol (although most of my favorites do or did, until those things just weren't enough to do the trick anymore). I don't believe I write better after drinking or doing drugs; it's just that experience has shown that I *actually* write after drinking or doing drugs. I call myself a writer but I don't write. Or at least I don't write what I need to, because the stuff I get paid to write is just enough for me to justify the label. Therefore, I actually can call myself a writer because I do get paid to write, and my byline has been read by a lot of people. But that's work. I put in the least amount of effort to churn out a product that is still decent by my standards. It's not always what I want to write about. I call myself a writer because I have several books, screenplays, sketches, and a million other things written...in my head. But in my head there is no rejection. No confrontation. In entertainment journalism—what gives me the occasional paycheck—there's nothing personal. There's no looking for answers. There's no cause, there's no let down, no consequences. It's safe. This weekend is not about being safe, hence the drugs and alcohol. It's time. It only recently turned midnight, so in the last 15 hours or so I've popped some Adderall, some Xanax, a few Stellas (that I picked up at a bodega before coming to this hotel so my habit wouldn't leave me with a regrettable mini-bar bill) and a quarter of a fifth of Johnnie Walker (I'm a writer; I don't do math). Yeah, I'm not Chris Farley or John Belushi because, contrary to the popular belief of those who know me, I do *want* to live. That's another problem. I want to LIVE. This hotel I'm staying in is in the fucking middle of fucking Times Square in New York City. Can someone please tell me who the fuck enjoys Times Square? It's because I want to live that, even though I was committed to sitting in here, drinking and writing, I left. I walked out of this hotel knowing very well what was outside. Tourists. Lots of fucking tourists. Actually, I don't hate tourists. I haven't been in New York for long, so I'm nowhere near native enough to talk shit. I just hate people. I am definitely native enough to this planet to know I hate people. I hate people and I hate crowds, hence the Xanax and the cigarettes. I'm actually not a smoker. That's the best kind of smoker to be, because a cigarette every now and then always does the job. I never picked up smoking because I saw my dad try so hard to quit in his late thirties. The guy was on the patch, the gum, and still smoking. Unfortunately, or fortunately, I never saw him during his struggle with alcohol (he's 30+ years sober). So…I pour it down my throat like someone lost in a desert coming to his first oasis. Every happy hour, every shot, every pint is an oasis from life for me. It's not like life is hard for me. I think most mature adult drinkers can admit that drinking doesn't really change anything. Here's what it does change for me. Like I said, I don't believe a writer must drink or do drugs to be good. But I must drink and do drugs to write. I'm not better or more creative, but I'm more in touch with my emotions. I've never argued that alcohol isn't a depressant. I've also never cared. What do we learn from the music and the books and the films that are about happy people? All of those things require conflict, heartbreak, and pain to deliver their message. I am not a bitter person…when I'm sober. I'm not a bitter person when I'm drunk either, but my mind is more in touch with The Shit. I'm a pretty happy-go-lucky dude most of the time. I also don't write most of the time. You know when I write? On the train after a long day and night of drinking. Or anywhere after a long day and night of drinking. That's just what works for me. Maybe one day the booze and the drugs won't do the trick for me anymore, and I'll go the way of some of my favorite writers.

But a bigger part of me feels that if I just write, if I just finish something, I'll be happy. There have actually been those days when happiness just seems so far out of reach that the easy way out seems appealing. There was a very short period in my life—like a few months that I slept through—where I'd take a couple of Ambien in the afternoon, even though usually one would do the trick, pass out, wake up at night and then take a few more to go right back to sleep. For this very brief (in the grand scheme of things) part of my life, I just wanted to sleep, and I didn't care if I woke up. I don't know if it was the height of my unhappiness, but it was more about the lack of options that the U.S. Army provides to escape that unhappiness. But as I mentioned earlier, luckily, I have that writer's ego that makes me think I'm too important to kill myself. This weekend, that is what is keeping me going. The world needs to hear what I have to say. Or at least that's what I think. And we've established that's all that matters…to me.

That was just *a* stupid thing, not *the* stupid thing.

This is stupid. I left work today a little later than usual. My walk to West 4th to catch the C train is only a few blocks away, not too far from the Hudson River, so usually by the time I get out of work, there is an enjoyable sunset over Jersey City. Today was no different.

It's been over a decade since terrorists flew those two planes into those two towers and changed everything about how we live. I was 18 when it happened. Still a kid…kind of. I was living in Austin, Texas with my best friends and bandmates at the time. Sure, we were all affected by it, but I think, for some people, the further you were from New York, the less it impacted you. Or maybe it was because I was a stupid kid. I really don't remember any period of time in my life where I had any kind of legitimate fear that I was in danger. At least not that kind of danger. Yeah, going through airport security is a pain in the ass, but I honestly can't recall any point when I had an actual fear of becoming a victim of a terrorist act. Again, and I never really thought of this until writing this, but perhaps it's all chalked up to the self-involved teenage mindset. But, you know, even on the 10-year anniversary of 9/11, living in Manhattan, I still felt perfectly safe and didn't have a worry in my mind other than getting a music review in to an editor. I would have loved to have gone to the memorial, but I avoided it—not because I was afraid of a terrorist attack, but because I was afraid of a panic attack from being in the crowd. But today, years after the most horrible day in my lifetime, it finally happened. I was briefly hit with that fear. And it freaked me out. Like I said, I've only lived in New York City for a short time, so I don't really know how things work around here. In the two years before I moved here, I probably visited five times, and I spent a couple of months up here for an internship a few years ago—so I'm not right off the bus, but I'm still learning some things. I left work in a bit of a different mindset because, rather than returning to my apartment, I was on my way to take advantage of luxury accommodations at the Times Square Renaissance Hotel for the weekend. On the days when I bust my ass at work, which is pretty much all of them, that causes a bit of anxiety in my fucked-up brain. And while I have a pretty good supply of Xanax, that shit makes me sleepy, unlike cigarettes, which will only give me cancer or emphysema. So, I took my time. I strolled the neighborhood I work in, puffing on my Camel (Crush, because I'm not a real smoker, remember?), watching the sunset over Jersey City, and just relaxed. Probably for the first time this week. That's when *the* stupid thing happened. Actually, this requires a little bit more of a preface.

Since I was determined to write this weekend, I started preparing myself early. Yes, I considered bringing a flask of whiskey to work and starting off early, but I made the responsible decision (which is rare for me), and I refrained from drinking on the job. I did, however, listen to sad bastard music all day. Booze, drugs, and sad bastard music get my mind and emotions exactly

11

where they need to be in order for me to write. And women. Fucking women (adjective, not verb). So the song that came on my iPhone while I strolled down Vandam towards my 6th Ave. subway, was Jimmy Eat World's "23," off their album *Futures,* which has always been my favorite Jimmy Eat World album. No, it's not because I haven't heard *Clarity*. No, I didn't discover Jimmy Eat World along with the rest of the world when "The Middle" hit MTV. I'm not trying to be cool by saying I heard *Clarity* first. You'll find that I learned early enough in life that I am not cool, therefore trying is a fool's errand. Here, let me prove it.

My discovery of Jimmy Eat World is something very, very, uncool, but it's partially to blame on the tiny town I grew up in with almost no exposure to indie music—or small bands, since *Clarity* was on Capitol Records and not technically "indie." As soon as I turned 18, I moved four hours north to Austin. That's the only cool part of the story. When I lived in Austin, I worked at a Hot Topic in Barton Creek Mall, the rich white kid mall (I lived in a two-bedroom apartment with four other guys). So I got to know Jimmy Eat World through my cooler coworkers at a yuppie mall's Hot Topic (not cool), but I *discovered* them when the song from *Clarity*, "Lucky Denver Mint," was on the movie *Never Been Kissed* (so not cool). So I've loved the band forever, but it's *Futures* that I keep going back to. The words to "23" aren't particularly relevant to this situation, the song just happened to be playing at this moment—that moment that, for a second, I thought could be my last.

"I felt for sure last night, that once we said goodbye, no one else will know these lonely dreams. No one else will know that part of me."

12

Not relevant to the situation, but I manage to always find a way to make songs I love relevant to my life. Actually, I'm pretty much an open book with those who get close enough to me. I just don't let many people do that. Even if I did, this city is not the easiest place in which to do that. I disagree with the New Yorker stereotype that says that this city is filled with rude assholes, but I really feel like no one here is trying to make friends. I think New York City is probably within the asshole-per-capita average. There are just more people here, thus, more assholes. One might draw the conclusion that it's possible that there are more nice people here, too. You just have to find them. Which means you have to look for them. And who the fuck wants to do that?

"You'll sit alone forever, if you wait for the right time. What are you hoping for? I'm here, I'm now, I'm ready. I'm holding on tight."

I get it. I've been alone for the better half of a decade now. Sure, I've dated plenty, had plenty of flings, but nothing that stuck. I have no idea what the hell I was hoping for, years ago, when I left the best relationship I had ever been in, with a girl who is still one of the best people I've ever met in my life. But…you move on. "I won't always love these selfish things," Jim Atkins sings in "23." "I won't always live…not stopping." That is exactly how I've lived for the last 10 years. Not stopping. I'm here, I'm now, I'm ready. I think. When I left that relationship, it was for one reason and one reason alone. There was no lack of love. There was no lack of attraction. I just wasn't there. I just wasn't ready to stop.

This was the song that was blaring in my ears as I inhaled the last breaths of tobacco, nicotine and whatever other poisons that were setting the foundation in my veins for their friends that would soon join them, and I looked up into the sky, and I saw a plane...flying low...over Manhattan. For that split second, I got scared. Actually, it was a good 20 seconds. It wasn't a real scared. I mean, I've had anxiety attacks just being in a loud crowd. This was more thought-based. I'm a pretty smart guy, so I try to logically work through things before panic sets in. But that's the shitty thing about legitimately having an anxiety disorder—it doesn't matter how smart or logical you are; that shit will sneak up on you, and it will knock you on your ass and take your wallet. Sometimes the fucked-up part of my mind skips right over being logical and jumps straight into panic mode, but this wasn't one of those times. I was ok. I'm not sure how long you have to live in New York to become familiar with the airspace regulations. In the few times I've flown into New York City before. Not once did we fly over Manhattan. And this plane was pretty low. It didn't help that two weeks earlier, during an office happy hour, while watching that Jersey City sunset, a coworker talked about watching from her office window as the second plane on 9/11 flew towards the second tower. I can't even pretend to understand what those directly affected by the tragedy feel like, but when she said that, it was something new to me. Most of us, the lucky ones, watched it happen on TV—myself from 2000 miles away, during that time I lived in Austin, right before clocking in at a Chic-Fil-A, where I'd spend the rest of my day getting updates from the occasional customer that popped in every 10-30 minutes. If you didn't watch it live, you've most likely seen it played over and over on the anniversary of the horrific event. But— and this can't just be my perspective—watching it on TV really just made it feel like watching a TV show. Still, to this day, I have not met anyone who lost somebody on that day in September 2001. So, it's hard to make it real in my mind. But when I heard my coworker's story, it got a little more real.

So, stupid as it may be, my heart sped up a bit when I saw this plane. I saw it fly over the Hudson, watched it disappear behind a building and wondered if I would feel it hit. Was Jimmy Eat World too loud for me to hear it hit?

"Amazing still it seems; I'll be 23. I won't always love what I'll never have. I won't always live in my regrets."

That was the mood I was trying to set for myself. Amazing as it seems, I'm 30 years old, and thanks to movies and music, I've romanticized this city for almost as long. And because of that, every time I'm in this city I fall in love with something I'll never have. But regrets are not something I struggle with. This city owns my heart, and every time I've been here, I've always been a visitor. I've always had to leave. But I'm here, I'm now, I'm ready. I live here now. I don't have to leave. Now whatever I fall in love with will be something I can have, right? Not just part of a short dream I'd inevitably wake up from.

That's what it was. It wasn't fear. The thoughts that entered my mind weren't, "We're under attack," or "I'm going to die." I thought, "God, please don't let this happen again to this amazing city." It was like seeing a friend go through one-too-many bad relationships. I don't know how much more she can take. Within this 20-second thought process—while I lost site of the plane and waited for the earth to shake—I also thought about my family in Texas. I'm not the best at keeping in touch with my little sisters who are still young enough to need their big brother around. I don't call my mom enough after that woman worked harder than anyone I know to make sure my brother and I knew we could go somewhere in life. I have a niece and nephew whom I could probably be more inspiring to, but definitely should check in with more often. I love

15

those kids and every time I get to see them—and they love me back. But what about when we don't see each other? I remember when I was a kid, I rarely thought of aunts and uncles who lived in other states or even the ones who just lived two hours away. Within that 20 seconds I was almost sure something horrible was going to happen. I didn't panic, I didn't run for cover. I grabbed my phone and thought, "get ready to dial someone and let them know you're okay." Because if you wait five seconds too long in those situations, it's too late, and everyone you love has the worst week of their lives worrying about you. I didn't want that happening.

It's strange how easy it is to feel alone in a city of millions of people. It's even stranger how no one tries to remedy that. I'm one of these people—the lonely and the lazy. I don't really know what to do about it. Today I legitimately thought, for about 20 seconds, that I was going to be directly affected by another 9/11—for the first time. I'm not paranoid. I fly a lot and I never fear my fellow passengers, no matter what they look like or what they're wearing on their heads. I think the real fear today was not that I haven't lived enough, but that I haven't loved enough. My main concern, in that 20 seconds it took to me to regain rationality, was my family. I don't want them to worry about me. I love them, and they know I do, even though I definitely don't tell them enough. I have given them plenty of reasons to worry (Xanax, Adderall, Ambien, Scotch) over the last few years. Maybe it shouldn't take a commercial airliner crashing into a building for me to call my little sisters to tell them I love them. But family's different. It's easy to call them up and say, "I love you." But the girl. *The* Girl. Yes, there's a girl. Isn't there always? She also worked her way into my mind during that 20 seconds, and it made me want to call her. It made me want to spend this weekend with her. It made me want to spend as much time as I could with her. We only have good times together. So why shouldn't we spend the weekend together? Why shouldn't we spend our lives together? Because you have to play the game. We've known each other for years, but we've never lived in the same city. And now that we do, somehow it's still not the right time. Or at least she doesn't seem to think so.

"You'll sit alone forever if you wait for the right time. What are you hoping for?"

I'm sitting in one of the nicest hotel rooms I've ever been in, in the middle of the greatest city in the country, some say the world, and I'm alone. See? I told you *this* was stupid.

"Tortures of the Damned" – Bayside

"I hate myself, more than I ever let on. I'm burned out at 22. I lived too fast and I loved too much and I'll die too young, but I chose this cup that I drank from. Knew what I was getting into. But I couldn't let out what I had to keep in. I'm ashamed of myself and unspeakable sins that I've committed..."

In my five visits to New York City, I had only stayed in a hotel one other night before. My best friend, Brandon, has lived here for a few years now, and I have always stayed with him because he was usually the reason for my visit. He is the only other person I've told this story to, and I don't think I told him immediately. The night I stayed at the Chelsea was a night that I was supposed to stay at his place. But, like many drunken romantics before me, the romanticism that led me to New York also led me to the Hotel Chelsea and its hallowed halls where Kerouac wrote "On the Road," and where Charles Bukowski lived and Dylan Thomas died. There was nothing romantic about my six or seven hours there.

"I've made mistakes, but I'll find my way. There's no explanation for, the things I've failed at before. They can't hold my hand. It just hurts to be a man, through the tortures of the damned."

It was my third visit to the "greatest city in the world"—fall of 2010. Brandon had been dating a coworker named Jennifer or something for a couple of weeks. I was happy for him because Brandon didn't date much. I was happy for me because his girlfriend would most likely have girl-friends, and that would save me the trouble of having to make my own during my short four-day weekend. The first day I met Jennifer, she brought along one of those girl-friends. I was warned, for whatever reason, "this one is off limits." I know the reason I was warned. Because, had I not been, I would've tried to sleep with her. I just don't remember the reason she was "off limits." Maybe she was in a relationship or had just gotten out of one, and while those things haven't always been a guaranteed deterrent for me, I heeded the warning, and just upped my charm so whatever good impression I made would be passed on to their friends who *were* available.

The four of us shared our Texas roots—which was more than enough to work with—as we shared mid-day beers at an Irish pub called Bull McCabe's in the East Village, where lonely middle-aged people had some sort of internet "meet-up" to play board games and not be lonely anymore. Isn't that what we were all doing? Brandon and Jennifer didn't have much in common and didn't last very long. For the short time they did last, they weren't lonely. I flew almost 2,000 miles to hang out with my best friend because at "home," I was lonely. We made friends with board game group, played some games, drank some beer, and talked about what a great city New York is. It seems like there's a period of time in which New Yorkers—or at least the transplants never tire of this topic, until all of a sudden, the opposite feeling takes over the soul and the conversation.

We were at that pub longer than any of us expected to be. Then, the events of that night blur together—until the end of the night, when everything slows down. I remember going to a comedy club and drinking whiskey-and-cokes. Part of that just might be because I always drink whiskey-and-cokes when I'm trying to not look like a drunk who prefers the whiskey without the coke. I know we had a good time because it kept going. Our next stop was another bar on the Lower East Side called Home Sweet Home, where we met up with more of the girlfriend's girl-friends. These ones weren't off limits, but I was off my game. It was the kind of dance club I actually enjoy—the kind where you can get lost on the crowded floor and have a good time without feeling like everyone is watching you, judging you. See, that small south Texas town that I grew up in, it had a few bars, but really only one that the college kids went to for a good time: The Country Luau. Despite its name, it wasn't just country music (which is probably my favorite genre to dance to anyway). You got the occasional "Hey Ya" or "Remix to Ignition" thrown in. But this was a town of 25,000 people, that I had spent most of my life in. It was the kind of town where, not only does everybody know everybody, everybody knows everything about everybody. And that was just too much pressure for me to ever get out on a dance floor. Turns out, I'm a pretty good dancer, so that fear I had of small-town judgement might have been irrational. But I didn't have that information until I moved to L.A. at 22—where I knew absolutely no one and absolutely no one knew me—and started going out to clubs, getting lost in those crowds, dancing, and having the time of my life.

That night, on the Lower East Side, at Home Sweet Home, that's what I did too. I drank and I danced. Then I drank some more and I danced some more. I made friends with the girl-friends, and I made them laugh. This was one of the more impressive periods of my life—I was in NYC to photograph and write about a band for a magazine that my brother and I had been running for years, and I was just about to open a comedy club in my hometown. So, it wasn't hard for me to appear as if I had my shit together.

So, I drank. And I danced. And the girlfriend's girl-friends took me in. But then the alcohol did what it does. Here's where the night slows down. Brandon had his girlfriend. The girl-friends had each other. The New Yorkers had each other. Not only was I the outsider, but I was the outsider with a fucking backpack on.

"If I only had an axe, I'd sever the ties I've made with this world. Maybe I could be a stranger, in a strange place. If I start now maybe I can be saved."

Surely there was another stranger in the crowd who was as alone in their head as I was. I mean, statistically that sounds right. But nothing knows the true definition of the word "alone," like a depressive mind. Wait. See, that's the thing. The *true* definition of the word "alone" is not the one that the depressive mind settles on. It's far from it actually. But it sure as hell don't feel like there could be a truer definition in that moment. I was an outsider to the of the club doors. What do you do when you're an outsider to the outside? If you can't feel at home at a club called Home Sweet Home with people from your home state, will you ever feel at home…anywhere?

Brandon knew he wouldn't have to worry about me when he and Jennifer left me there. I've never had trouble holding my own with women. So, he was right to not worry.

The circumstances under which Brandon and I met are actually kind of interesting. He and I both came up in the same music scene back in Texas. We both played in bands, and our bands even played shows together.

21

We may have met in Texas, but it would've just been in passing. I certainly don't have any memories of us hanging out in Texas. Years later—five years after I stopped *playing* music and had begun working in it, to be exact—Brandon and I both wound up in living in Nashville. He had gotten his degree and was working the kind of job where he had to wear a tie and most of his coworkers were older than him. I had spent the previous two years in L.A. trying to write, drinking, partying, and sleeping with girls who were way out of my league. After those two years, the relationship with my best friend/writing partner in L.A. had run its course, and for some reason, the aforementioned girl who was the best girl I ever dated still liked me. She had gotten a great job in Nashville, and after a four-year-long on-and-off relationship with her, we decided maybe it was time to be "on" again. When she asked me to go to Nashville with her, I saw that as a way out of L.A., where I wasn't very happy at the time. This is apparently what I do. As a skater-punk lead singer of a ska band, I wasn't very happy in the tiny town in south Texas where I grew up, so I left it as soon as I could and moved to Austin when I was 18. By 20, I had a falling out with that band and moved back to my tiny hometown to give college a shot. At 22, I got restless, remembered what I realized four years earlier—that I didn't fit in or belong there—and I packed up all my shit and moved to L.A. Two years seemed to be my limit in a new city, and my two years in L.A. were up.

I had passed through Nashville before while on tour with my first band and thought I liked it enough to relocate, even though a few of my bandmates had gotten robbed in a WalMart parking lot. The guys got caught a few miles away, and since the getaway driver was apparently the police chief's nephew (from what we were told), we got on the news. The good citizens of Nashville who recognized our very recognizable school bus that we toured in, stopped at the venue that we were playing at and gave us money. So, because of those great people, and the great restaurants and music scene, Nashville just felt like Austin. Or so I thought.

I packed up and made the move. I was wrong about everything that led me there. The relationship only lasted a couple more months, and living in Nashville is definitely much different than visiting. At least it was for me. I was working at a small independent record label where I was a booking agent for indie singer/songwriters and Americana bands, and no matter where I was, I constantly found myself surrounded by people who felt like they were all authorities on music. While I am a music nerd, I've never felt like an authority. I like a lot of music that many people hate, and I hate a lot of music that many people like. Even when I write about music, I rarely say that something is good or bad. I say, here's what I like about it, here's what I don't like about it, you should check it out and see for yourself. I never found my place in Nashville, but I suppose since I gave it less than a year, maybe I didn't give that city a fair shot.

Needless to say, I was unhappy there. And lonely. After a few months of living there, a group of old friends from my music-playing days back in Texas came to visit. I jumped at the chance to feel some familiarity—to get the chance to relive the last time that I can really remember being happy. Since Brandon was also a part of our collective past, our mutual friends invited him out too.

One of the nights that we hung out, we visited some touristy bar on Broadway and had some drinks. Broadway is the tourist Mecca of Nashville. Or maybe Times Square is a more appropriate comparison, since there is actually quite a bit of Holy Ground in Nashville if you're a true music nerd, and it sure as hell ain't on Broadway. Except Ernest Tubb's Record Shop. Broadway is where you'll find themed bars and the Hard Rock Café. Maybe it was a weeknight, or maybe we were just so lost in nostalgia that we didn't care about the tourist element. After all, I suppose my friends were tourists. It was the second night we were all out together, so I still didn't know Brandon very well. As we all sat at a table drinking and chatting, we noticed Brandon at the bar talking to a girl. Good for him, we all thought. A few minutes passed and he returned to the table...alone. We asked what happened, and apparently, he was interrupted by a friend of the girl he was talking to. A tale as old as time. Now, as I said, I didn't know Brandon all that well, but I don't need to know a guy well to help him achieve whatever noble goal he might have with a pretty lady. I've had some pretty good wingman experience in my day, and I've learned from some pretty good wingmen, so, and I shit you not, I said, "I got you." I got out of my seat, and Brandon and I walked back to the bar and back to his girl and her friend. I occupied her friend with what could've been interesting conversation or complete bullshit, I don't remember. What I do know is that Brandon got a phone number. I didn't. I don't think I even asked. I wasn't there that night to meet girls; I was there to hang out with friends who made me feel at home, and with those people, on that night, I wasn't lonely. A funny thing happens in those situations. It really is loneliness that leads me to meeting women. The same thing happens when I go to concerts. If an important concert is coming up, I exhaust all of my resources to ensure that a girl that I like is standing next to me while watching a band that means a lot to me because I want that moment to mean a lot to me. But it doesn't always work out that way. Sometimes, the invitations go out and the answers I want don't come back in. But what am I supposed to do, not go to the concerts? So, I've found myself at plenty of those important concerts alone, and it's never mattered once I'm there. The people in those crowds—singing along every word with me—become my friends. If those songs mean as much to them as they do to me, we are family.

That night, maybe Brandon was still lonely. I'm not sure. We've never talked in-depth about where either of us was in life then. I think just because we've always been able to relate to each other so well through the years, there's just an understanding of where we were. Now, when that night comes up, it's only looked back on as a funny flicker in our past like many nights that followed it. We had many similar nights in Nashville and many more in New York and even in Austin over one crazy drug-and-booze-fueled Austin City Limits Fest weekend. After that night in Nashville, our mutual friends returned to Texas, and Brandon and I became best friends. I was only in Nashville for another few months, but we made the most of that time. We both lived within walking-distance to that same tourist main street made up of flashy honkytonks. No matter how much we despised all that strip stood for, we frequented it looking for ladies, and when we couldn't find them, we'd start looking for fights—looking to feel something different from whatever it was that we were feeling. I'm not sure what the ratio was, but I like to think we were fairly successful in the former, thus avoiding the latter. Needless to say, we were always drunk.

I was always Brandon's wingman, and for the most part, I was always the one who initiated the conversation with women. I had no problem with that. However, to his credit, he got better at it. Brandon knew that if he and I were going to drink and hit the bars, we were definitely going to at least talk to women who would at least feign interest in us. I had just failed at dream chasing in L.A., and at a great relationship, and Brandon wasn't quite happy with his station in life either—so feigned interest from women was sometimes all we needed to sleep at night. That might have been the early foundation of our relationship, but since we had some background and self-loathing in common, our foundation got pretty solid. We've both gone through some crazy life changing experiences that have moved us all over the country, we've both gone through some nearly-debilitating depression, and we've been there for each other through it all. I even stood next to him as his best man on his wedding day, years after those Nashville days. But that's another story.

Another thing that I think has kept our friendship so solid is the fact that we have both been the embodiment of the saying "wherever you go, there you are." After Nashville, I moved home to south Texas where I've never been happy, and Brandon moved to New York and pretty much fell back into the life he led in Nashville before we met. He was in a better city—this city, the "greatest city in the world"—but he was still lonely, still in the same work environment, still drinking a lot and still having trouble making friends and meeting women. As for me, I found myself in almost the same lot, but in a worse city. I wasn't having trouble making friends or meeting women, but I was having trouble making friends and meeting women with whom I saw a future. So, while our friendship was only kept alive through the occasional phone call, email and my visits to New York, it still stood the tests.

So, when Brandon and his girlfriend left me in that bar in New York with a group of girls, he probably thought it could only work out well for me. I suppose that's relative. I don't know if I ever talked to the other girls again after Brandon and his lady left. I wasn't ostracized by the group. I was ostracized by my alcohol-addled, prone-to-depression, fucked-up brain. Maybe I could've gone home with one of those girls that night, but because Brandon had already done so, I felt like I had failed. I felt like my time was up, the game was over, and I fucking lost. All of a sudden, the music was too loud. All of a sudden, the crowd was too big, the room was too small, the girls were too pretty, and I was too alone. I had to get out.

I didn't tell anyone I was leaving. Maybe I was afraid that they wouldn't protest. I walked out onto Chrystie Street, walked around the corner, and sat on the sidewalk where I had fully intended to sleep that night. For some reason, this has been my instinct under similar circumstances before. I remember almost sleeping behind a small brick wall in Kingsville, Texas, after a fight with my brother. One night when I was around 24, I looked for a safe place to sleep in the streets of Los Angeles after I had walked three of the five miles between my apartment and the bar where another friend had left me. A few years later—but not any more mature—after getting in a drunken fistfight at a Washington D.C. hotel party during my time in the Army, my friends found me in an alley, where I went to escape the anxiety and just…sleep.

"I've made mistakes, but I'll find my way. There's no explanation for the things I've failed at before. They can't hold my hand. It just hurts to be a man, through the tortures of the damned."

But that same little voice in my head that says "have another drink," also says things like: "Fuck it. Get up, get a cab, and go to the Chelsea." It didn't say go to a hotel, it said "Go to the Chelsea"—the exact words I told the cab driver.

$139 a night? That's a small price to pay to sleep in the same building that some of my heroes had slept in. I paid in cash, got my key and went to my room. At this point in time the Hotel Chelsea looked like the kind of place where Dylan Thomas died of pneumonia. It looked like the kind of hotel where Sex Pistols' bassist Sid Vicious's girlfriend Nancy Spungen was found stabbed to death. But I was drunk and depressed, and the Hotel Chelsea looked like the kind of place to be drunk and depressed, or get drunk and depressed if you weren't already.

When I got to my room, I turned on the TV and flipped through the channels. I swear to God, I could not make this part up: the Jason Segel/Paul Rudd film "I Love You, Man" was on. On the night my best friend leaves me behind with strangers at a bar to go home with his girlfriend, I end up drunk and depressed in a sleazy hotel watching a movie about two male best friends. That was too much. I couldn't be alone anymore.

"Look at me now I'm on the tracks with my back towards the last train leaving town."

It had to be 4 a.m. by now—that's when the bars close in New York, and I left before closing time. I walked downstairs to the hotel lobby to pick up a Village Voice. Brandon and that Hotel Chelsea front desk clerk are the only ones who know what happened next. There's most likely only one reason someone in a hotel picks up a city's alt-news weekly at 4 a.m. What good were live music listings and drink specials now? All the businesses in town were closed, except for those advertised in the back pages—escorts, massage, "company."

"Look at me now I'm on the tracks with back towards the last train leaving town."

I didn't spend too much time looking at the pictures next to the phone numbers. I was drunk, I was lonely, but I wasn't stupid. I had never paid for sex before in my life, but like a delicious-looking hamburger in a McDonald's ad, I was sure that there was no way that the product would live up to the advertisement.

I don't remember if there was an answer at the first number I called, but I remember that I invited the first answer over. "How much for the whole night?" I asked, as if her answer would affect my response. "$300." I gave her my room number. She had to come from Brooklyn, which meant I had to wait. I don't remember how long I waited, but I do remember I watched that whole fucking movie, which probably played a big role in keeping me from changing my mind.

"I've made mistakes, but I'll find my way. There's no explanation for the things I've failed at before."

There was just a knock at the door—no call from the front desk or anything. It's probably better that way. If this particular woman had checked in and given them my room number, I wouldn't even want to face strangers who could link me to her. Of course, this is all in hindsight. The Chelsea really was a sleazy hotel, and I'm sure she wasn't the first hooker to come through the lobby that night, nor I the first lonely bastard who made the call. However, it's not a cheap sleazy hotel, so she might have been the least attractive. I want to hold on to a little pride here and say she wasn't that bad, but she was. I want to say she was "slightly" overweight, but, again, I'd just be trying to save face. Her skin was dark. Maybe she was black, but like a Caribbean-kind-of-black. Throughout the more-than-a-decade since I lost my virginity, I had never been with a black woman. I don't choose to hook up with white and Hispanic girls, it just so happens that I have hooked up with more white and Hispanic girls than any other ethnicity. Actually, I've hooked up with way more white girls. I remember when I was in high school my Mexican mother made fun of me to her sister because every time she checked the caller ID it always had "white" last names on it. But that's just how the dice have rolled. I grew up mostly around white and Hispanic girls, so I've hooked up with white and Hispanic girls. Every one of my girlfriends has been white, though. Wow, I just realized that now.

There was this one girl, when I lived in Nashville, that I hooked up with a few times. She was half-black. She was beautiful and had amazing breasts. But she was also awfully naïve for a woman in her mid-twenties. The first time we hung out we ended up making out in her bed like junior high school kids—Drake Bell poster on the wall and everything. She said she wouldn't have sex with me unless I was her boyfriend. All of a sudden, I was her boyfriend. Just like that. And I was actually momentarily committed to it at that moment. Or I at least momentarily kept an open mind. Then, after I left, I called her and said, "I think we moved too fast." We "broke up." When a few days passed and I wanted to fuck her again, "I miss you" and "let's try it again, I don't know what I was thinking." Yes, I was an asshole. Sometimes I still am. But there I was, in a sleazy hotel with an unattractive woman who I paid to have sex with me. Karma was getting me back.

This woman was objectively unattractive. As I look back on it, I realize my drunkenness really kept me from registering immediate self-hatred or disgust, but I can still picture her clear as day. She didn't even make an effort to look nice. I guess in her professional experience, if a guy is calling at 4 a.m. from a sleazy hotel, you probably don't have to look good. I can't remember what she was wearing, but I can remember she did not look nice. Hadn't she ever heard "dress for the job you want, not the job you have"? I don't know if she had any rules about not kissing on the mouth, but she had a set of jaws that made any such rules unnecessary. And I remember all of this. Or at least I think I do. Perhaps my brain is just painting a picture that perfectly personifies the shame I have from the experience. That could be very possible.

Had I been driven by anything but loneliness and depression, I might have turned her away when she got there. Had I been sane, I might have thought, "this is a bad idea," paid her fee and sent her on her way. But she arrived, and I was no longer alone. I was no longer lonely, and all I had to do was give her $300. What a deal!

I invited her in. It wasn't like the movies. I wasn't nervous. I wasn't scared or unsure of how to talk to her. We both knew why she was there, so we didn't waste time with bullshit. And when it was all over—not an embarrassingly low amount of minutes, but definitely not enough to justify the cost—I was sane again. Or, I had at least somewhat come to my senses. I was still lonely, maybe more depressed. I thought to myself, *that* was a bad idea. Not that I was scared—hooker or not, I always wear a condom. But I've never had a lot of money, and I immediately thought, fuck I've spent over $500 tonight. I don't remember any conversation, if there was any. I do remember that she started by going down on me. Maybe this is weird, but I'm not particularly a fan of that. I think it's probably about a 50/50 chance that I can keep going after finishing like that. I suppose the dignifying thing (if that's at all possible in this situation) to have done would have been to let her finish, then just have her hang out until I was ready to go again. I paid for the whole night, you should have to be on duty the whole night. But I made her stop, and then I got started. I'm sure I wasn't thinking that the sooner it was over the sooner I could get her out of there. If you're a man, or know men at all, you know that rationality doesn't set in until after the deed is done. The haunting vision is much clearer now than it was that night, thankfully. That night, I was clouded by

31

loneliness and drunkenness, and, yeah, depression, and that's fine with me. When I think about it, it seems like Vietnam. If I had been completely present in the moment, I wouldn't have been able to perform my duty. Now I'm just haunted by vivid flashbacks. She didn't stay the whole night. I didn't want her to. An old pro like her probably expected that—buyer's remorse. She was maybe there for 30 minutes. $10 per minute. No wonder it's "the oldest profession." She went back to Brooklyn, I went to sleep.

I might not be happy about what happened in the six or seven hours I stayed at the Hotel Chelsea. But I am happy I stayed there before it was purchased and shut down for renovations. The Hotel Chelsea will never be the same, and neither will I.

"It just hurts to be a man, through the tortures of the damned."

"Settle Down" – The Dangerous Summer

"I gave my things away. I called the people that I only see on holidays. This next year's gonna burn a hole in me."

The Times Square Renaissance is not the Hotel Chelsea—all the comfort that the original Chelsea lacked, and none of the history. So much has happened in the years since that disgusting night at that disgusting hotel. Maybe that night was my rock-bottom. How far away from it am I now? This hotel is nicer but the brain is still just as messy, my blood just as poisoned, actually more so tonight— Adderall, Xanax, scotch. I'm still lonely, still depressed—but I don't have $300 to spare tonight. Even if I did, the one girl I want here tonight writes for magazines—she's not advertised in the back pages of them. I've been here before.

    This might get morbid. I've never been deliberately suicidal. There was that short period when I was in the Army—I really didn't care to live because I was so miserable—that I abused pills, and in the real way, not the fun way I do now. I've always thought that I love my family too much to ever cause them the pain that comes from a suicide. So, while I really didn't care if I died in my sleep, I wasn't trying or hoping for it. I just wanted to sleep. I never set out to kill myself. My ego probably deserves some credit there. I know how much potential I have. I just have to figure out how to reach it.

I've had more freedom than anyone in my immediate family, so, really, I could never justify such a selfish act as suicide. Not only that, but I know my older brother has been in an unhappy marriage for more than 10 years, and he has the responsibility of raising two children and running a business and a household. So, if I were to take that "easy way out," I really wouldn't have a valid excuse, being a single guy who has always had the luxury of being able to chase his dreams no matter where they led. I also remember some pretty tough times growing up poor, with my single mother trying to raise two boys and eventually a baby girl who came along, all while she was trying to finish school and working minimum wage jobs. My mom's situation hasn't changed much. And now, that little sister and another one are still dealing with the same lower-class lifestyle that my brother and I escaped as soon as we were legally (and financially) able to. Then there's my brother's kids, who see their parents fight, hear them argue, and don't have any way to escape it. The thing that has kept me from suicide has always been the thought of the pain that it would cause the kids in my family. A close second are the statistics that show that if you kill yourself, it's more likely that someone else in your family might choose to do so as well. And just about everyone in my family has more reasons to do it than I do. But isn't that relative? Feeling like the "easy way out" isn't available to you sure doesn't decrease your motivation to take it. Perhaps some more scotch will help.

"I spend my weekdays in my car and my weekends drinking hard enough for two."

Anyway, back to the morbid part. This is kind of a suicide note. Kind of. Again, I haven't deliberately set out to kill myself. Life is actually going pretty well right now. But I've had a lot to drink. I've also been uppin' and downin' all day. My Texas comedian friends and I call that "Belushing." As in: John Belushi. You know, the guy who died from mixing uppers and downers. So, I'm a bit Belushed right now. Xanax and Adderall and booze. Who knows where that's going? In fact: Another Round!

I'm getting a little tired, which makes no sense to me with the amount of Adderall I've taken throughout the day. But there is an amazing king size bed behind me, and it would probably be pretty ridiculous to not take advantage of it while I'm here. When this weekend is over, it's back to the air mattress that I currently call a bed. My original intention was to pop Adderall after Adderall and stay up for three days writing. Doesn't look like that's going to happen. I should probably finish this, since it appears, so far, that I am committing suicide. Well I'm not. If I don't wake up tomorrow…oops. This will stay open on my computer so anyone who cares will know it was an accident.

"I feel the weight of the world on my back…"

I remember, while I was in the Army, I read an *Entertainment Weekly* cover story about Heath Ledger's death. I think it was the year anniversary or something, and they had interviewed several close acquaintances. It was originally speculated that his death was a suicide because he had prescription drugs with him, but it was ultimately declared an accident after mixing the wrong combination of drugs. When I read that, it clicked. Maybe Ledger wasn't *trying* to kill himself either. Maybe he was so miserable, like I was at that time, and didn't want to feel anymore or be awake to experience it. Maybe he just wanted to escape his misery at any cost, even if that cost was death. That thought crossed my mind back then, and I still popped more Ambien to sleep away the misery. And when I would wake up, I took more, along with painkillers, over-the-counter cold pills, and booze. Lots and lots of booze. I didn't want to die, but I most definitely did not want to live under those circumstances. I wanted to be somewhere else. And sleep was the only "somewhere else" I could be. A permanent sleep was kind of appealing.

"I laid awake in bed, and thought of better times. I never want to sleep, 'cuz I've found apathy in laying down and never waking up."

That's not *the* morbid part. *The* morbid part is that I could die tonight. I've had quite a bit of Adderall (upper), Xanax (downer), and all washed down with scotch and beer. The pills started off at work, but that's a normal workday for me. I need the Adderall to get through the day and stay focused and get my work done. Before certain meetings, like one we had today, and if the work starts piling up, I have to take some Xanax so I can calm down and avoid anxiety attacks. Then there's *The* Girl. There's always *The* Girl. We had an amazing date two days ago, but every time we hang out it's amazing. So just thinking about her gets my heart racing. This weekend I have this hotel room overlooking Times Square, and all I could think about was sharing it with her (more Xanax). So when I got off work, I formulated the plan. And this is just me being stupid. I'm usually pretty cool. I don't need plans and I don't play games; I just need to learn how to slow down (more Xanax). *The* Girl is another story for another time. I just took a Ambien. I've only got a few minutes before I'm incoherently rambling, and a few after that before I pass out in place. Now where were we?

Oh yeah. In case I die tonight. I love you, guys! Yeah right, I'm going to go out on something that generic? I know my friends and family know I love them, even if I don't tell them enough. My mom should know she's the strongest person I know—was, and still is, an amazing mother. Maybe I didn't reach my potential, but I've done some amazing things that I couldn't have without her constant encouragement. I've kept going for her.

Sometimes my little sister doubts my love for her because I haven't been around enough. I moved out when she was eight. But, as clear as day, I remember babysitting her when I was 12 or 13, and I would cry when we watched *Barney* and this "You're My Sister" song came on. I'm crying now just thinking about it. My youngest sister is one of the coolest girls I know—and one of the strongest people I've ever met. She's been through so much crap with her parents (our mom, her dad) than most of us will in a lifetime and she's barely a teenager. It blows my mind when I see that she has held on to stickers from my old band for 10 years. That band broke up when she was two. She has always looked up to me, and I definitely haven't earned it. She reminds me a lot of myself at her age. She wears the clothes she wants to wear, listens to the music she likes, and doesn't care what anyone else thinks. And she gets made fun of because of it. But she keeps going. She's obviously much stronger than I am. My Mom and my sisters are all smart and they're all beautiful. I hope they're lucky enough to avoid asshole guys. I've kept going for them.

My nephew is my brother's son. He's probably the smartest person in our family. If he keeps it up, he'll be the one who saves us all (no pressure, kid). He's also the most well-behaved kid I've ever seen in my life. He's a great nephew and is going to be an awesome big brother to his little sister. She's the dangerous one. She's either the most evil kid in the world or the cutest kid in the world. Is that wrong to say in an "in-case-of-suicide" note? But the cute times make the evil times worth it. Better? She's definitely the prettiest girl in our family, hence the danger. But her big brother will take care of her. (I want to sleep. But what if I don't wake up?)

That little girl is going to be pretty and charismatic enough to be a "mean girl;" I hope she stays as cool as she is now—always laughing and being goofy. Do any of us stay as cool as when we were children?

I can't express how much I love my dad. It's funny because a few years ago I couldn't express how much I hated him. There were some pretty bad moments in the last year that I wouldn't have made it through without him. Moments like now, when the Ambien is kicking in and I'm not sure if I'll wake up tomorrow.

"I laid awake in bed, and thought of better times. I never want to sleep, 'cuz I've found apathy in laying down and never waking up."

I wish I could say this is the first time I've considered impending doom. As I said before, I wasn't too excited about life in the Army. I do have that whole book written in my head, too, so I'll save the bulk of the story (drugs, booze, suicide attempts, more drugs, more booze, and more suicide attempts) for when I'm a better writer and when I'm ready to revisit the worst experience of my life. The relevant part of my short military experience is that I drank more than I ever had before as a south Texas high school or college kid, more than I had in two years as a bachelor in Los Angeles, more than I had in the previous years as a stand-up comedian and music journalist. I was also doing way more drugs than I ever had. It helped that the U.S. Army will pretty much give you any drug you ask for if you know how to ask for it. "My ankle hurts." Here's some Percocet. "I can't sleep." Here's some Ambien. "I'm depressed." Here's some Klonopin. And if you didn't have what you liked, someone else did, and pills were the new baseball cards. If you still couldn't find the high you needed, you just walked to the store and looked for it in something you could get over the counter. I was 25 years old when I did my first "whip it." I put an aerosol can of computer keyboard cleaner to my mouth and sprayed. It was a 10-15 second experience that just made me dizzy and blocked out all other noise with this echoing sound of a light saber pulsing in my head. I wouldn't even call it a high. I decided it wasn't worth the brain cells it killed and I never did it again. Maybe I did it once more right then just to confirm. Triple C's—cold, cough, and congestion pills—usually did the trick if you had eight hours to lie around and stare at the light on a smoke detector. I tried it all, and most of the time mixed whatever I could get and washed it down with alcohol.

At one point in that mess, my mom's mom was dying back in Texas. I'd be lying if I said that bothered me. She really wasn't a loving grandmother to my brother and me. It was the phone calls from my crying sisters that made me want to be home. My grandmother eventually passed, and I couldn't be there for them. Maybe it wasn't a big deal to anyone, but in my already-depressed mind and unhappy life, it just added to the pile. So, I took more pills. I drank more booze. And I slept. I took four Ambien to sleep through the day, and when I woke up I'd take four more to sleep through the night. Then one day I got a phone call from my mom. I never called my family because I didn't want to worry them. And I often ignored calls from them. But this time I answered. It was right around the time I read that *Entertainment Weekly* Heath Ledger article. My mom told me that she had a minor heart attack. When I asked when, she said almost a month had passed, but she didn't tell me because she was already worried about me. So, I decided to get my life together. Well, I decided not to die anyway.

"I think I'll settle down one of these days. Till I catch my breath, I feel the weight of the world on my back, But I'm not feeling sick to death."

The second time I was spared came after I got out of the Army and ended up back in Corpus Christi, going back to college and running a local comedy club with my brother. He and I have really only been good at working together for about six months at a time. Our six months at the comedy club were up, and they ended with a big fight.

In almost three decades, we've had a lot of fights. One of them even landed me in a holding cell for three nights. I had just moved back to my hometown from Austin, where I was living with my band. We had just returned from what ended up being our last national tour, and I decided I needed some space. So I went home and lived with my brother and his family. One night, he and his wife were having an argument, like many nights before and after. This one was getting particularly ugly, so I decided to step in and try to calm things down. Bad idea. Well, I suppose the result I was looking for did come. My brother stopped arguing with his wife, but started arguing with me. This is another one of those nights that is kind of a blur until everything slows down at one moment. I can say that there were no drugs or alcohol involved. I was only 20 at the time, and believe it or not, I didn't start drinking until 21. So maybe these days I'm just making up for lost time. I don't know what was said or by whom that night, and I don't know how the confrontation became physical. I just remember that, at one point, I was on the ground with my brother on top of me. Now, my brother only has two years on me, but in our adult lives he's always had at least 100 pounds on me. So, when I'm on the ground and he's in control, I'm pretty much done for. To his credit, he has never beaten me up. I can't even recall a time when he has even punched me. I can, however, remember a time, when we were kids, that I hit him over the head with a skateboard. I don't remember what we were arguing about or what made me think that I needed to do that. Maybe I was just being a shitty little brother like little brothers can be. Why he never beat my ass, I will never understand. And this time was no different. He was probably just subduing me until I calmed down. I didn't see it that way then. My instincts kicked in and I reached for the first thing I could grab—a metal bass drum pedal—and I hit him on the head with it. That's when things slow down. No. That's when things stop. I saw blood coming from my brother's head and I seriously thought I had just killed him.

I wish I could get sentimental here and list all the amazing times he and I had, and how those memories would result in some kind of huge regret. But, to be honest, I don't have a ton of great memories with my brother. We hung out a lot as kids, but it always seemed to be a burden to him. Sure, I guess having to take your little brother everywhere could be a pain in the ass, but he had cooler friends and they did cooler things. I do remember that, at one point, when we were growing up, my brother finally misbehaved enough for my mom to fulfill the threats she had made for years. She sent him to live with our strict, retired-Navy dad 14 hours away in Oklahoma. I remember I cried a lot at the airport and stood by the window until his plane took off. That was back in the day when you were still allowed to do that. I remember standing by those floor-to-ceiling windows and trying to see my big brother's face through those tiny rectangle windows on the side of the plane as it rolled away. I wonder if he has any memories of that day. I never really think about that day, but when I have, I've never considered what he might have been feeling. Was he scared? Was he full of resentment towards our mom? Did he worry about me at all? Maybe I should ask him sometime.

He was only supposed to go for three months. I remember thinking that three months sounds too long for me to be without my big brother, and so does 90 days. But, in my mind at the time, if I looked at it as 12 weeks, for some reason, that made it a little easier for me to deal with. When those 12 weeks were up, my brother didn't want to come back. I'm not sure what it was that made him make that decision, but he stayed in Oklahoma, 14 hours away from his little brother, for over a year. And you know what, I honestly don't remember what that year was like without my brother. Maybe if I really thought about it, placed it in the timeline, remembered where I was at that time, I could probably figure it out. But off the top of my head, I can't. Now that I think about it, this is the first time I've ever considered how my little sister—10 years younger than me—felt when she yelled at me, crying, about not being there for her.

And there I was, my brother hovering over me with his blood dripping on me. I felt really bad about it. That counts for something, right? He got off of me and I ran outside, where the police were waiting. Apparently, his wife had called when we started fighting. And when you live in a small town where nothing's going on, police response time is pretty quick. Through my sobbing, I told the police what happened so that they would call an ambulance. I wasn't crying because I was hurt or afraid of the cops. I wasn't either of those things. I was crying because I thought my brother was going to die and it would've been my fault. He turned out to be fine, but that didn't change how horrible I felt. It also didn't change the fact that I was getting arrested. My brother didn't press charges, but when you commit "assault with a deadly weapon," the city can press charges on you. So, I went to jail—to a holding cell actually. And there I sat. Freezing. My bail was set too high for any of us to afford. Two nights passed before I finally decided to let my dad know what happened. He wired bail money, and on the third day I was out. "This is the only time I will ever do something like this for you," he said. Understandable. Whether he meant it or not, that's exactly what a dad should tell his son in that situation.

The second time I could've killed myself (accidentally)— nearly 10 years later, while no blood was shed and no one ended up in jail, it was still the worst fight we've ever had. We had been working together, running a comedy club in our hometown for a little over six months, when he just took it over and push me out. It was something I worked really hard on, something I invested a lot of money in, and something that finally made me feel like I had some purpose. And then it was just crushed. It hurt me in way that I never thought someone in my family could. And he enjoyed it way too much. With the loss of that "something," there was the loss of our brotherhood that had weathered divorce, assaults, distance, and differences. It was a pain that lasted weeks for me, but the night it happened was one of the worst feelings I've ever had.

I'm lucky that this was something that I got over in a few weeks. I'm extremely lucky that I was even given another day. It happened on a Friday night. I had just gotten home to my apartment after a comedy show at our club. Some comedian friends were in town for the show, and we all had an after party at my apartment along with some friends and strangers. Doesn't really sound like the setting for a suicide story, does it? Hey, John Belushi and Chris Farley weren't trying to die either. I got a phone call from my brother, and after arguing a little bit, tried to return to the party that I thought would take my mind off the bullshit. I can't really remember whether or not I told people what was going on. I just remember thinking that I couldn't let them see how upset I was. So, I drank whiskey. Or, I drank some more whiskey. Friday night comedy shows were always stressful to me. Not only did I run the place, but sometimes I also had to host and make sure the comics and audience were taken care of. So, there was already a night full of whiskey and Xanax running through my veins. What would a little more hurt? Maybe nothing, but on top of the cocaine I had done and continued to do by myself in my room—behind a closed door that was usually open to anyone who wanted to partake—I was laying the foundation for an unintentional tribute to some of my comedic favorites. A line here, a shot there, some Ambien once I ran out Xanax, another line, another shot, and I was out.

The next evening, I woke up. I had slept for 15 hours. It wasn't the first time I had been careless with my life, but it was the first time I had written a "just in case" note. It was scribbled in blue marker on the dry erase board in my room where I usually wrote things like "email publicist about interview" or "turn in assignment." That evening the only thing written was "If I die it's my brother's fault." It was written in the scariest scribble, like I had written it with the wrong hand, or like a child just learning to write took his marker and wrote on the wall while mom wasn't looking. I didn't remember writing it. I don't remember writing it. I remember reading it the next day and being very scared. At least a year passed until my brother and I said any words to each other that weren't designed to hurt one another. And, honestly, that year was one of the best years of my life. I got healthier, accomplished some things that made me feel better about what I had lost, and I moved on. I wish I could say that's all I needed. I got healthier, not healthy. Come on, who doesn't almost die once or twice a year?

"I think I'll settle down one of these days."

"Poison In My Veins" – Bayside

"The night sky's black and I'm awake lying on the ground. The grass beneath my feet is hard and cold just like I've come to be. The stars are gone behind the clouds and I can't see a thing. So I'll just let my eyes stay closed just like me, I can't open up."

So, I woke up today—in that king size bed, in the Time Square Renaissance. I'm not upset about that at all. Like I said, I've never wanted to kill myself. And yesterday wasn't even a depression or misery thing. Well, maybe it was a little, because of *The* Girl. And, you know, "*The* Girl" doesn't even really mean one girl in particular. I mean, right now, it means one in particular, but if I weren't here in New York this particular girl wouldn't be *The* Girl. I'm sure some other girl would be. Even if I were at a particular point in my life where I didn't know a girl to be *The* Girl, the idea of *The* Girl is enough to drive me to the drink and the drugs. Jesus, I just woke up and I already sound like a drunken rambling buffoon (my morning Adderall should fix that right up). It doesn't necessarily take my mind off that idea, but it helps my mind turn that shit into something.

"There's something in an empty bed that makes it hard to close your eyes. It can eat at you until they both turn black and blue. And all you want is a reason you should live or a way for you to die, a way for you to die."

I thought about calling my family today. After writing that in-case-of-suicide note last night, I thought a lot about how much I love those folks, and I thought maybe I should call and tell them. But then I started drinking. Of course, that was after my morning amateur speedball (Adderall and Xanax). I had a nice morning glass of Johnnie Walker and then realized that there was a coffee maker in my room. So, since I declared this weekend a "work" weekend, and I never start a work day without coffee, I made myself a cup...and poured some Walker in there too. My mind was scattered for a few minutes before the drugs kicked in. Take a shower, go get food, write, drink. Do I need to take a shower? I'm in a hotel room and I don't plan on seeing anyone for days. I *need* a drink. I *need* to start the day with a drink. Focus. Pour yourself a drink, then everything else can happen after that. Should I go get food first and bring it up and drink with my food? Just drink! Then you can go get food, bring it up, and drink more with the food. Great idea. But I need to take a shower. See, if I were a junky, would showering even be on my priority list? I don't think so. So, I took a shower with a shower beer: compromise. And I hit Times Square to grab some street food—from a street vendor, not a street trashcan—and wander around.

"Cause I'm all wrong, and I don't see a chance to fix this head. So just give up. Write me off, pretend I don't exist."

I eventually came to the Playwright Tavern, a "Celtic" pub. It looked exactly like a Celtic pub should, and they had Smithwick's on tap, so I pulled up a barstool, and ordered my pint. It was still only about 1:30 p.m. and I was well on my way to drunk. Thanks to a double of Johnnie Walker. By 3:00 p.m. there was no more "on my way" about it. I had reached my destination. I was drunk. But, like I've said every time I've defended my alcoholism, I can do this today. I don't drink at work. I don't call out sick from work when I'm hung over, nor do I go to work drunk or hung over. In fact, I've been told by my boss on multiple occasions how impressive it is that I can be out drinking until 4 a.m. and still be at work the next day on time, looking professional and staying on task. That is, until the day I came in after our open-bar Christmas party with my face smashed up like it had been dragged across a rough concrete sidewalk. A smarter more professionally-minded person might have said he had gotten mugged, but not me. I let everyone know that when I got home, I dropped my keys, leaned over to pick them up and just kept going. My face hit the rough concrete sidewalk outside of my apartment. I had a lot of tequila and Johnnie Walker that night. But, the next morning, I got up, cleaned my face wound a bit and I went to work, which is more than I can say for some of my superiors who were just hung over and didn't even show up. I keep my responsibilities and fulfill my obligations. To me, that separates the addicts from the abusers. Yes, I abuse drugs and alcohol, but only when it's okay to do so. I'm in a luxurious hotel for the weekend, on someone else's dime. I don't have a wife or kids who need my attention. Should I sit here sober and sad that I don't have anyone who would be affected by my actions? Or should I sit here drunk and sad that I don't have anyone to share it with? No brainer.

I walked out of the Playwright Tavern—which I would not recommend to anyone looking for Celtic pub experience, unless your idea of a Celtic pub experience is Beyonce blaring over tourist talk. But I can't complain about the $7 double of Johnnie Walker. How that cost less than my pint of Smithwick's makes absolutely no sense to me. I walked out of the pub and straight into a gift shop. When you're in Times Square, it's actually more difficult to *not* walk into a gift shop. I still hadn't stopped thinking about my family, and still hadn't stopped thinking that I could've died last night. Man, wouldn't that just make everything so much easier? But I was too drunk to call my teenage sisters or my recovered alcoholic father just to tell them I love them. They would suspect I was drunk. Not that it matters to me. Well, it kind of matters to me. Like I said, as long as I fulfill my responsibilities, I think I'm doing alright. But my dad has been brainwashed by AA for over 30 years, and still believes he can't have one drink. So calling him would just make him worry. My sister just doesn't understand the real world yet, and because of things my brother (who also has never had a drink in his 30-plus years) has told her, she thinks I'm an alcoholic. So, while the most burning thought in my head at the moment was, "I just want to tell my family that I love them," I couldn't do it. So, I looked at post cards. Maybe I could just send them post cards. I thought of my niece and nephew and how I really want them to have better lives than my brother and I had. I want to send them post cards that show them how amazing this city looks. I want to spark their imaginations. I want to inspire them. I want them to believe that they can get away. I'm also drunk, and probably tweaking a little bit since I doubled up my morning dose of speed. And who knows what the hell scotch in coffee does to you? So, I decided that children do not need to receive the drunken ramblings of their crazy uncle who has never been the most stable guy they've known— sober or not. Oh shit, I'm *that* uncle.

"The ground's opening up. I'm falling down below – an endless fall into a place that I don't think a child should know."

7:00 p.m. came as quick as my alcohol buzz went. I was getting tired and had plenty of work to do. So, I put a pause on the drinking, and tried to pep up a bit with a little more speed. I've definitely tripled my daily dose today. Possibly more, since I came in to my room earlier to pop a pill, but within 30 seconds couldn't remember whether I took it or not. I couldn't find it anywhere, but I knew for a fact that I had not ingested any liquid. So, did I just throw it down my throat, or did I drop it on the floor? I assumed I threw it down my throat. I wish I had some cocaine. Actually, I've wished I had some cocaine all day. For some reason that seems to do the job better than Adderall. A poor workman blames his tools, right? I guess I'll work with what I've got.

"It's the poison in my veins, the poison in my veins, the poison in my veins that got me through."

The Girl #1 – "Megan" – The Smoking Popes (Covered by Bayside)

"Butter on a summer day, when she's around."

The Smoking Popes' song "Megan" is a great song about the kind of love that can drive someone mad. Isn't that only kind worth having? It's also a pretty simple song to play on guitar, and that's the only kind of songs I can play on guitar. The funny thing about The Smoking Popes is that I used to listen to them when I was in high school—probably around '98-'99. I remember hanging out with these really cute soccer girls—one whom I'd eventually end up dating—and somehow they were into some really cool punk rock. Now, sure, it's not weird for high school kids to be into punk rock, but I'm talking about a small town of 25,000 people in south Texas. We had to try really hard to find good punk, and even semi-popular bands like Smoking Popes were obscure where we came from. Somehow, these cute girls, 2 grades above me, knew who they were. I also remember listening to bands like Zoinks and Squirtgun with them. Why they took me in, I don't know. I'm glad they did, because if they hadn't, I might not be the person I am today. But as years passed, I have to admit, I forgot about the Popes. It's not that I ever strayed from that music. I never felt like I had to listen to anything else to be "cool." I think it just had to do with how difficult it was to get that stuff in Kingsville, Texas. Bad Religion, Pennywise, Voodoo Glow Skulls, that stuff was a little easier to hang on to. But

I lost Zoinks, and I lost Smoking Popes. So, it took Bayside's cover of the Smoking Popes' "Megan" to bring them back to me.

I wanted to fall in love the way the singer of this song had with his Megan. I wanted to play my "Megan" this song, and have her fall in love with me in the same way. There are no great songs about Michaels, are there? Maybe my "Megan" would write one.

"Butter on a summer day, when she's around. I was on the tracks when the gate came down. Suddenly I recognized those blood-shot rear-view mirror eyes as mine. I heard that whistle call my name, I almost drove away...But Megan, I had a feeling that you would be on that train, so I just waited there for you."

Here's the beginning of the story about Meghan (but with an "h") and eventually the end. You already know the middle. It was the same trip as the infamous Hotel Chelsea—my third trip to New York City in two years. Although those trips may only add up to about two whole weeks, it just seemed to be the place where I belonged—definitely more so than that small beach city I retreated to when I got thrown out of the Army with nowhere to go. Corpus Christi was my home because that's close to where I grew up, and that's where my family moved to when they left our small hometown, Kingsville. It was the "city" 45 minutes away from the tiny town where I spent my childhood. It was where we drove to catch shows, go to a real mall, and it's where my friends and I would go when we cut school to get certain CDs on the day they were released. Corpus Christi was never a place where I felt like I belonged. New York City kept calling me back, and I kept answering. Every time I had visited, I had fallen in love with the city, but every time I visited I wanted to fall in love *in* the city. As a product of pop culture, I live to experience real moments like the ones in films like *When Harry Met Sally* or *Sleepless in Seattle*. There are no movies in which those magical moments happen in Corpus Christi, Texas. I'd like to think that maybe someday I'll write one. But they say write what you know, and I don't know about anything magical happening there. So, I was convinced that those moments couldn't happen there, or at least not for me. They can and do happen in New York City. This is the story of the first time I fell in love *in* New York City. And in August of 2010, I met *The* Girl #1, Meghan.

"Caught a ride to another town where the air was clean and the sun never goes down. Everyone was standing in a line between the landing and the stairs. I heard somebody call my name. I almost climbed the stairs. But, Megan, I had a feeling that one day you'd meet me there. So I just waited there for you."

Brandon had been dating Jennifer—the girl with Texas roots and cute friends—for maybe a couple of weeks. The funny thing about being semi-charming and initially good with women is that it kind of becomes your party trick. Since the day we met in Nashville, Brandon has taken a little too much enjoyment in sending me on missions and challenging my "talents." Sometimes I crash and burn, and sometimes I'm Maverick.

I was in New York for a four-day weekend right before the first semester of my return to college in the fall of 2010. I met Jennifer on the first night, within an hour of landing, when my cab dropped me off, luggage-in-hand at a Brooklyn music venue. I wouldn't have it any other way. The band was great, and when they finished, Brandon and I went to his apartment, and if memory serves correctly, Jennifer went back to hers. But not before we all made plans to meet up the next day. Saturday started off as wholesome as possible, but, as you know, ended in a completely opposite way. Brandon and I grabbed brunch, which is a New Yorker's excuse to start drinking before noon. I like the way they think. I never needed an excuse, but, hey, I'll take one. After brunch, we met up with Jennifer and the off-limits girlfriend at the Irish pub where we drank, played board games and drank some more. I stuck to my plan of being charming and funny, and I waited. It's almost easier to impress a girl when there's no reason to impress her. So, the off-limits girl was just practice for when we would eventually meet up with their friends who were available. And later that night, after the Irish pub and comedy club, but before the Hotel Chelsea, we did meet up with them. And there was Meghan.

I'd be lying if I said I picked Meghan from the beginning. I was just a dude in New York looking to get laid. I know, I know, I said I've always wanted to fall in love *in* New York, and here's the thing: I fall in love far too easily. If I'm going to sleep with a girl, I usually convince myself to fall in love. Maybe it's just for one night, maybe a week, maybe four years. I love women. I love sex too. There's a great band called The Format—the former band of the lead singer of Fun.— and in one of their songs there is a line, "I love love. I love being in love. I don't care what it does to me." And that is exactly how I approach any woman who might appear to have the least bit of potential. On this night, I was with a group of them.

We met up with Meghan and her friends on the way to Home Sweet Home. She worked in fashion and so did her friends. Like Jennifer, Meghan and her friends also had Texas roots. So, we were all clicking. Like I said before, that night is all a blur of drinking and dancing, and eventually the depression that led me to the Hotel Chelsea. The problem with love is that no matter how much you love it, you can't make it exist—unless, apparently, you have $300. Then it appears real quickly, and disappears just the same.

When the weekend was over, I found myself exploring New York solo while Brandon was at work on Monday. It was my last full day in New York, and I hadn't been able to shake the depression. Surely that wasn't anything a few pints of Smithwick's couldn't help. I wandered into Twins Pub, another Irish place with a real Irish bartender who talked about her fantasy football team and didn't mean American football. This is why I love New York. Sure, I was alone, but a simple accent, great beer and good conversation already made it a way better place to be alone than Corpus Christi—where I'd be flying back to in less than 24 hours. It was my last day in the "greatest city in the world," and I didn't know if or when I'd be back. I did, however, know that Brandon and I were to meet back up with the girls from Saturday, and I was determined to get my game back. I still hadn't told Brandon what had happened on the night I didn't come home—at least not the whole story. It was my own little shameful secret. In fact, I think not bringing it up helped me block it out like it never happened.

Time flies when you're getting drunk. Before I knew it, it was time to move on to my next destination: Eastville Comedy Club. This time, I would not be an audience member, but I'd be taking the stage during an open mic night. I had been doing stand-up for a couple of years, and had even done a couple of theater shows in front of a few hundred people. But I never felt comfortable doing it. I have absolutely no desire or delusions of becoming a famous stand-up comedian. It's just always been something I did to keep my writing fresh. And like any other kind of writing, it's something that I can do on my own without the worry of anyone else ruining it for me. When I had played in bands, it was never my idea to end them. No matter how close we were to success—and sometimes we were pretty damn close—someone else always managed to kill that dream for me. But stand-up and writing were things I knew I could do well, and no one could take them away from me. Stand-up comedy is not easy, and it's especially not easy for someone with anxiety disorder. This was pre-Xanax prescription, so before doing a set anywhere I'd write my own prescriptions—Vicodin, tequila, whiskey, cocaine. I remember one night—well, I don't really remember it but I know it exists—I was performing at a theater in Corpus Christi at a sold-out show of around 400 people, and I used just about anything I could to make me forget about the anxiety. The part I do remember is when I headed over to a buddy's apartment, popped some Vicodin and washed it down with quite a bit of whiskey. Then, I'm pretty sure there was some cocaine in between that and getting to the theater, where there was unlimited Patron. That's all I remember. I know that I went on stage as an opener who was only supposed to do 5-7 minutes. Twelve minutes later, and after bumping into some prop comic's table on stage, I stumbled off stage committing the ultimate stand-up sin: stealing time from the other comics. But, I do remember someone at the afterparty telling me I was the funniest person that night. Whether it's because they were laughing with me or at me, I didn't ask.

So, on this day in New York, before going up on stage in front of a bunch of New York comics, my prescription was a few Irish ales and quite a bit of whiskey. That would have to do. Brandon met me at the comedy club, where he was the only one in the crowd who wasn't a comedian waiting for five minutes of stage time. Having a friend in the crowd always makes it a little easier for me. I did pretty well. I know I have some sure-thing jokes, and while the purpose of an open mic is usually to test out new material, I was there to test out my material against a crowd of comics. And not just any comics, but a crowd of New York comics. For me, doing stand-up is a lot like my writing. I put a lot of thought into what I'm going to say, so I'm always pretty confident that it should work when it comes out. Doing well at a New York comedy club in front of a crowd of New York comics is the best medicine for any lacking confidence that might ail someone approaching his last chance to fall in love (or get laid) in New York City. I left the comedy club a new man; I'd still be my charming old self, but I just conquered a room full of some of the most judgmental people you can face. A table full of Texas girls would be no problem.

We met the girls at a Mexican restaurant called Maracas. Chips, salsa, margaritas—I felt right at (wait for it…) home. I sat across from Meghan, and honestly, that was probably when it hit me. Not out of convenience. I wasn't weighing my options. I was just there to have a good time with good people. And whatever happens happens. And it happened. It was the first time I got to look into her eyes. They were almost as green as mine but just enough on the grey side for me to fall for them. As far back as I can remember, women have told me I have pretty eyes. I've never argued with them, but I've disagreed in my head every time. Until now. Meghan had beautiful eyes, and her dark hair made them pop. I was done.

"Butter on a summer day, when I hear that name it's a dream that never came true. Sat down on the tracks and waited for a train to take me back to you. Somebody came and took my hand. I finally had to go. But Megan I just want you to know I waited as long as I could."

She was cute, she was funny, she was confident. Finally, I was falling in love *in* New York City.

56

"Butter on a summer day when she's around."

The night was turning out much like two nights before: Brandon had Jennifer, the off-limits girl had the other off-limits girls—only this time, I had Meghan. Enough of a foundation had been laid on Saturday that I was approved by everyone, so the night just went on. After a few margaritas and some more getting to know each other we all decided that we would find a karaoke bar. There are only a few things in this world I can do to impress a woman. I don't have a lot of money, and I'm not particularly good at sports. I can usually talk or joke my way out of a fight, but that's only a good skill to have when defending yourself, not when defending a damsel in distress. I also have a pretty good sense of direction, but how many girls have that on their list of things that make a man sexy? I'm also not delusional about where I stand on the looks spectrum. I'm a decent-looking dude, not super-hot, but definitely not unattractive. I could probably be in better shape, but I've definitely aged gracefully. But now I was at a karaoke bar. Put me in a karaoke bar with a lady, and it's over. Once that decision was made, Meghan's fate was sealed. Whether she knew it just yet or not, she would be going home with me and we would be testing the durability of the twin-sized air mattress on Brandon's kitchen/living room floor. Not exactly the romance of the movies, but it's more about the event than the circumstances under which it takes place. Right?

Meghan and I talked all night, and every new piece of information ended up being something else we had in common. We both grew up listening to the same punk and ska bands. We both came from religious pasts that led us both into not-so-religious futures. And, most importantly, at that moment, we both loved karaoke. She could sing, and she wasn't afraid to. That, to me, is very attractive. I swear, and I tell this to every girl who says it: ninety percent of women think they can't sing, their car is a mess, and their apartment is a mess. These are statistics I've gathered over years of research. I'm not saying that ninety percent of women can't sing or have messy cars and apartments, just that ninety percent of women seem to think those things. But Meghan was confident, and that's one of the sexiest qualities a woman can have. And having her eyes definitely helps.

She sang Lisa Loeb's "Stay." Of all the songs, with less than 12 hours until a plane takes me back to Corpus Christi, Texas, she sings "Stay." Yes, I overanalyze music. Yes, I make songs mean something even though they don't always mean something. I guess it's like the song says, "I only hear what I want to." And right then, at that moment, I wanted this beautiful, confident, funny woman to just ask me to stay. So, at that moment, that's what I was hearing. It was time for me to respond. Jack Kerouac once said, "Don't use the phone. People are never ready to answer it. Use poetry." I've never been much of a poet, never really tried to be because I never really cared to be. I think the best poems have already been written. They are the songs we hear every day, the songs our parents played for us and that we will play for our children. So I used poetry, drunk on Japanese beer in a Manhattan karaoke bar. I sang The Cure's "Just Like Heaven." It was one of the songs my dad used to listen to so much that it's the first one that I associate with the memory of him playing records. Maybe it's because of that that the song has always been one of my favorites. I definitely heard that song way too young, but I'm sure I never understood what it was about back then. Nevertheless, it's a karaoke crowd pleaser. Other songs I also heard often when I was probably too young to hear them: "Runaround Sue" and "The Wanderer" by Dion and the Belmonts. "Runaround Sue" is pretty much about whore who cheats and sleeps around with every dude she can, and "The Wanderer" is pretty much about a man-whore who actually drives "around the world" to bang every chick he can. I'm guessing it's Sue's fault that the once-optimistic crooner who sang "Dream Lover" eventually became "The Wanderer." Those songs have also become go-to karaoke songs for me. And like "Just Like Heaven," they are karaoke crowd pleasers. But on that night, I was only trying to please one person. I don't know if she heard music the way I did—analyzing every line, understanding every word as if it were written in that second just for her. "'Why are you so far away?' she said. Why won't you ever know that I'm in love with you?" Before the song was over, she was right next to me, singing along.

As the night moved on further in an obvious direction, the two off-limits girls called it a night and headed home. They knew their friends were in good hands. Brandon and Jennifer were still there, but I don't think we noticed. Meghan and I were lost in conversation, the songbook, and in each other. Before we knew it, Brandon and Jennifer had disappeared. I think there was a part in both of us that wanted to keep the night going because we knew it would be our last together. I realize now that I really wasn't concerned with just getting laid. This was exactly what I wanted. I wanted to connect with the kind of girl that I didn't believe existed at "home." We drank more. We talked more. We attempted to sing songs that we only kind of knew—finding out that no matter how much you feel like you "Must Have Done Something Right," it doesn't mean you'll know that Relient K song any better than you actually do. We did anything to keep our night from ending. Finally, we sang one…last…song: Dashboard Confessional's "Hands Down." It's one of the best love songs about this kind of love—the new, exciting, awkward love that is scary because it feels more real than we've been taught we should allow.

"My hopes are so high that your kiss might kill me. So won't you kill me? So I die happy. My heart is yours to fill or burst, to break or bury, or wear as jewelry. Whichever you prefer."

I was hers. Sure, she was mine too. But when that dream takes over, you're no longer in control. All I could do was hope that she was as deep under whatever spell I was under. Was she thinking the same thing? Did she see me as confident? I mean, I'm sure I seemed to be, but by this time I was scared to death. I liked her. A lot. Did she like me? Of course, tonight she did. But, "Will you still love me tomorrow?" Another song I probably shouldn't have heard at such a young age. And what about when I go back to Texas? This isn't how the movies end. In the movies, when the people fall in love, they stay in love, but they also stay in the same city. I stopped worrying, and I kissed her. That was all it took. Within what seemed like seconds we were in the back of a cab heading back to Harlem, and Brandon's apartment, and my twin-sized air mattress on his living room/kitchen floor.

"The words are hushed let's not get busted. Just lay entwined here, undiscovered. Safe in here from all the stupid questions. 'Hey did you get some?' Man, that is so dumb.
Stay quiet, stay near, stay close, they can't hear.
So we can get some."

It was a perfect night. Later, Brandon would tell me that Meghan and I weren't exactly "hushed." But he's my best friend, he knows me. He knows what that night, what that girl, meant to me. It wasn't a conquest. It wasn't something to cross off my bucket list. It was proof that a dream exists. It was life breathed into an idea that, for some, is only in the movies. Or only in songs. For me, it was in real life.

"Hands down this is the best day I can ever remember."

That's the line. That's the reason that was the last song we sang that night. When I got back to Texas, Meghan and I talked on the phone a few times. Sometimes for hours, about nothing. We talked about TV shows, and music, and work. I told her about the song "Megan" and that maybe someday I'd play it on guitar for her. I even attempted a few times to record a video of me playing it for her, but I was never pleased with the results. We talked about seeing each other again, even though I think we both knew it probably wasn't going to happen. After a few months passed, Meghan made a trip to Austin. From what I gathered, she ran into the ex she left behind but never really left behind. We lost touch. But that one night was all I needed to believe.

"Another Travelin' Song" – Bright Eyes

"Well I'm changin' all my strings. I'm gonna write another travelin' song. About all the billion highways and the cities at the break of dawn.
Well I guess the best that I can do now is pretend that I've done nothing wrong. And dream about a train that's gonna take me back where I belong."

I call myself a writer, but I'm deathly afraid of writing. That is to say that I'm deathly afraid of writing anything of meaning. As I've said before, I'll review your band, your album, your film, your TV show, whether or not I like it or you. That's easy. I've been doing it since I was 18. Cameron Crowe did it as a kid, Neil Strauss started at 18, too. If it wasn't easy, do you think kids could do it? It's *this* shit that's hard. And, actually, it's not that it's hard. It's like the difference between telling the person you're dating, "I like you" versus "I love you." It's jumping off a cliff. Scratch that. It's the difference between telling the person you're dating, "Yeah, I like the band Bright Eyes" versus telling that person, "I love you." That's how the level of difficulty varies. Writing for real scares the hell out of me. But…I have to do it. Even now, this stuff, it's all bullshit. It's a fucking journal of one weekend of debauchery—a weekend of lonely, depressed, sad overindulgence. Of all the pills I've taken in the last 24 hours, none of them were my prescribed anti-depressant. Before writing that sentence I got up, poured some Walker in a glass, broke an Adderall pill, and grabbed some Xanax. I want to stay up (Adderall) and write (scotch) and calm the fuck down (Xanax). My heart hasn't stopped racing all weekend. Sure, that's probably the Adderall, but it's also *The* Girl. It's always the fucking girl. She and I had an amazing date just three days ago—an amazing date that ended with an amazing kiss. But I haven't really heard from her since. I'm in one of the nicest hotels I've ever been in: The Times Square Renaissance—18 floors above Times Square...alone. (Those pills aren't gonna take themselves.) Tonight, I am the reason hotel windows do not open.

I knew I was going to be alone this weekend. Of course, I hoped for the best, but in my life I've learned that I'm rarely that lucky. Three days ago, I was that lucky. But, you know, I have my music, my booze, my drugs and, now, a few pages of bullshit. But it's a start. See, I do have more important things to say. I have my book about the Army that I want to write. But *that* is really scary. The consequences of that book are just too heavy for me to approach it. When I write it, it might be the most important thing I'll ever do in my life. At least to me it will be. It has to be—not just for me, but for all the kids going through the shit I saw kids go through. But, I'm scared. There's a book written in my head about love. But it doesn't have an ending. I'm scared to start it because I'm afraid it will go on forever. I can write on and on about the women I've fallen in love with. I fall in love far too easily. But that's the adventure of it. I've had more than my fair share of one-night stands or two-week relationships, but I've convinced myself I was in love with all of them—for whatever amount of time they lasted. Well, almost all of them. Okay, some of them. Or at least I tried my hardest to. Sure, there was that period in life where I was just a dude trying to get laid, and while there's plenty of fun in that, even a fling is more fulfilling when there's some emotion behind it—until it's all over. But, like I said, that's another book. Or hopefully someday it will be.

I call myself a writer because, well, I do write, but also because almost every second of every day I think about writing. I think about it and I fear it. I don't call myself a smoker. I do smoke every now and then—usually after a long night of drinking. So, I guess it makes sense that, throughout this weekend of nonstop debauch, I've smoked like a fucking chimney. I do own cigarettes, but I lived a very long time without actually buying cigarettes for full price. I used to tell myself I'd never buy a pack of cigarettes in New York since they're like $13 a pack, and, after all, I'm not a smoker, right? See, here's how I get my cigarettes. At almost every music festival I've been to, Camel has had their promo tent set up. While they're main goal is to push their dip product, Snus, on you, they also give you coupons to purchase packs of cigarettes for only $1. My first encounter with this awesome marketing experience was at South by Southwest in 2009, or maybe 2010. Back then they gave you two free packs of Snus and two free packs of cigarettes. But apparently some law changed and now they're not allowed to hand out free cigs anymore. They can, however, still push that bullshit Snus out all they want. They're way around this was the $1 coupon, which you could redeem immediately in the tent, or hold on to for use at any store. And you could go back every day to stock up. At the weeklong South by Southwest, I usually stock up for the year. But just in case, I also make sure to stop by the tent at the three-day Austin City Limits Fest, and every other festival where I might see one. Nevertheless, it's free or close-to-free cigarettes. So, even for someone who's not a smoker, it's a pretty sweet deal. I'm also the most considerate smoker, because I'm not a smoker. I step away from anyone who might be annoyed by it, and if I can't, then I blow my smoke up towards the sky or in the most-polite direction. I don't mind being inconvenienced in order to smoke a cigarette because I don't *need* to smoke a cigarette. Except sometimes I do. I started smoking more when I was taking algebra and economics classes in college. Six months from graduating, and I had put those two freshman courses aside because, like writing, I am deathly afraid of math. Unlike writing, I will never use those bullshit subjects again in my life. Because I was not up to date on my Xanax prescription, I would smoke a cigarette before class to calm my nerves. It worked like a fucking charm. I suppose that's how people get addicted. I've always been pretty in-control of my vices. Booze, no problem. I quit for two months to get in shape for the Army. I sobered up for 110 days while I was in the Army. I can stop when I want to or need to stop. Cocaine: same thing. I've done it at parties, I wish I had some right now, I like to have it if I'm doing stand-up, but I've never gotten addicted. There have been crazy nights where I've found myself surrounded by strangers I just met that night, staring at a dinner plate with a mound of coke on it—to be shared by a lot of people, not just me—and there have been times when a gram has sat in my drawer for weeks because the right time to do it hadn't come along yet. Love is my drug, and that's the worst one, because no matter how much money you have, you just can't buy it. And once you've had it—and I mean the really good shit—you just want it all the time. And if you can't find it, well then you might as well be a heroin addict with no heroin. The withdrawals are fucking painful.

"Now I'm hunched over a typewriter. I guess you call that painting in a cave. And there's a word I can't remember and a feeling I cannot escape...

And now my ashtray's overflowin', I'm still staring at a clean white page. Oh and morning's at my window and she is sending me to bed again. "

I've been in this hotel for 32 hours. Or, I checked in 32 hours ago, but really, I've only been outside for about four of those. I'm a contest winner—this weekend of luxury was my prize for being the best concert photographer in a nation-wide contest sponsored by Nikon and Live Nation (thanks, guys). I can't afford to drink in bars around here, or buy nice dinners. I actually brought a microwavable dinner with me. I left earlier, because this is New York and you can find a dollar slice of pizza anywhere. But, you know what? I turned my back on three street vendors because their hot dogs were $3. It's not that I don't have $3. I do. But I'm not going to pay the price of a pack of hot dogs for one hot dog. It was a principle thing. As I predicted, a few blocks away I got two slices and a diet coke for $2.75. I grew up poor. I have some money right now, and I've had jobs where I've made more money than my mom ever has, but I can't imagine an amount of money that will ever change my mind to one that spends money frivolously. I had two goals when I checked in 32 hours ago: Drink every drip of scotch in this Johnnie Walker bottle and write. I came here to do two things: drink some scotch and kick some ass at writing (I'm a writer, not a fighter), and I'm almost out of scotch. My goal is 50 pages. I think I can, I think I can, I think I can (Adderall). But 12 hours ago, I didn't "think I can." You know why? *The* Girl. It's always the fucking girl. I caved today, and I texted her. And for the third time in two days, she didn't respond. So, I knew I would eventually have to address *her* in this story, and *she* is real. *She* is important. *She* is scary. I call myself a writer because I don't waste my time on bullshit. If I'm going to write something, it's not so it will be published, or so I will make

66

money off of it, but it is so it will be read. What's the point of writing something if not to be read? Do the sane among us sit at home only speaking to a mirror? No. If you have something to say, it is useless without ears to hear it. The great writers will tell you not to write to be published, write because you love it. I'm not sure I love it. I need it, that's for sure. I don't love going to work, or going to sleep. In fact, when I play that game where you pick a superpower that you would have, my superpower would be the ability to always feel rested without ever needing sleep. Currently, when I need sleep, I get sleep, but I never feel rested. Anyway, I don't write to be published, I write to be read.

But today, I got scared. So, when I went out for lunch around noon today, I took my time. I avoided, in every possible way, my purpose. And once I returned to my hotel, I became a smoker. I became a chain smoker. I was a bit anxious because I knew once I rode that elevator up 18 floors I would have to sit down at my computer and I would have to write. And, eventually, I would have to write about her. So, I lit cigarette number one, and I stood at the edge of 7th Ave. staring at the larger than life "Big Bang Theory" ad, the four or five giant Guess Jeans billboards, and a picture of Daniel Radcliffe that is the size of the building it is on, until my cigarette burned out. Then I lit cigarette number two. An NYPD cruiser pulled up in front of me and I wondered, even with my normal considerations taken, if I was in the wrong place. This city has some strange rules. I kept puffing as to fully sell the ignorance plea I would honestly use had I been approached by the officer. But she wasn't there for me, so I kept puffing and listening to my sad bastard music as I poisoned my brain into the proper depression required for me to write the way I want to, and I poisoned my lungs and whatever else by sucking in the sweet chemicals of a Camel

Crush. And then there was one. It was my "lucky" cigarette, flipped upside down and as alone in the pack as I've been in this hotel all weekend. Who came up with this idea of flipping a cigarette upside down when you open a fresh pack, calling it lucky and saving it for last? Once you've smoked it, you're out of cigarettes. That doesn't sound like very good luck to me. Nevertheless, even though I've never been superstitious about anything, I've always done it. I've always done it, and every time I get to that last fucking cigarette I think, alright, asshole, don't let me down. I can't recall anything great ever happening after smoking that last one. Here I was again, staring at the open end of a Camel Crush staring right back at me— thinking, prove me wrong. Give me hope. Give me the luck I need to finish this book, to let it be the answer to all my problems. Maybe it's that stupid way of thinking that has gotten me in this mess in the first place—hope, luck. If I get myself into all this pain and self-doubt, isn't it my responsibility to get myself out of it? But it's my lucky cigarette. What was I supposed to do, not smoke it? Go upstairs and write? This is how I came to the conclusion that I am deathly afraid of writing. Rather than face my fear and do the thing I live for, I hid from it and chose to do something that could literally kill me. It was less scary to me to overdose on the most poisonous legal drug in our country than to get my shit together and write. But it did make me consider donating money to cancer charities in case I ever need their help. So, I guess that's something positive.

"So I will find my fears and face them. Or I will cower like a dog. I will kick and scream or kneel and bleed. I'll fight like hell. To hide that I've given up."

The Girl – "What You Know" – Two Door Cinema Club

"I can tell just what you want. You don't want to be alone. You don't want to be alone. And I can't say it's what you know, but you've known it the whole time. Yeah you've known it the whole time."

The singer of one of my favorite bands, Two Door Cinema Club, began their peppy-pop-dance-rock song, *What You Know*, with a slowed down solo, acoustic croon of the chorus before the band jumped in to pick it back up. I was watching the Irish band for the fourth time in a year, and *The* Girl was standing right next to me. I was in New York City, watching one of my favorite bands, and standing next to a girl I've wanted to stand next to for years. This is why I believe what movies sell me, because sometimes those moments really do happen. Unfortunately, the messages that music sends us are also too-often true to life.

I told *The* Girl that my plan for this weekend was to lock myself up with a bottle of scotch and just write. It really was. I wasn't trying to sound cool or artsy or anything. This really is the most I've written since I moved to New York. This is really what it takes. It would be amazing if she was ignoring my texts all weekend because she knows how depressing, thus inspiring, that would be to me. I acknowledged the cliché of the writer, the scotch and the hotel room, but it seems to be exactly what I needed. Probably could've done without that "in-case-of-suicide" moment. Wish I could say it was the first. Wish I could say it will be the last. It's like falling in love with all the wrong women: you can't only expect to experience good feelings, ups without downs. I'm an emotional extremist. I love with everything I have, and when I hurt, well, unfortunately, it's also with everything I have.

I checked in to this hotel thirty-something hours ago, and while I'm in the hub of the city that never sleeps, I had no interest in it. I opened my curtains to a giant billboard of P. Diddy, admired the bustle below, and then got into writing mode, which, like I said earlier, I had been preparing for all day. I write better when I'm depressed. I get depressed better when I'm alone and when I drink. So, I got to work. Or, I tried to. The room, the view, the bed, the shower, the scotch, it was almost perfect. Something was missing. *The* Girl. It's always the fucking girl. Sure, when I check out of this hotel and this debauchery induced depression, I'll be happy that I sat down and wrote—something I haven't been able to do for months. What if she were here? No depression, no drug abuse, sure, but no writing either. There would be a whole different kind of happiness when I check out of here—a real happiness. Honestly, or at least I think, I could never write again if I had *her*. And this "her" isn't this specific girl, but *The* Girl. The one that is the "one." Yes, after all the years, all the heartbreak, I still believe in that. If the heartbreak in music exists in real life, why wouldn't the love of the movies?

"In a few weeks, I will get time to realize it's right before my eyes. And I can take it, if it's what I want to do. I am leaving, this is starting to feel like it's right before my eyes. And I can taste it, it's my sweet beginning."

The Girl and I have known each other for years, and, for years, there has always been a little bit of a flirtation. But we haven't exactly been right before each other's eyes. We've stayed in touch, but there have always been thousands of miles in between us. Within a few weeks of my move to New York the flirtation finally lead up to that kiss that, for me, was at least four years in the making. It wasn't only the culmination of years of curiosity, but also the result of a great night together. Even if it had been a first date between strangers, it might have ended the same way. The next day she sent me an email that said we couldn't get "involved." I understood. It wasn't the right time. She was far into her career and life that had been long-established, and I wasn't the most stable just yet. There was also some other personal bullshit that she was dealing with. I was just hoping I was good enough to make her forget about that. But I didn't stay in touch with her for four years because I thought or hoped she was "the one." I had no intentions or expectations. I stayed in touch with her because she's one of the coolest girls I know—beautiful, smart, funny, and nerdy in all the ways I can appreciate (80s-90s pop culture, music, not Harry Potter and video games). Yes, I am attracted to her in all ways one can be attracted to another. Yes, even as relationship-phobic as I am, I would consider myself very lucky to call her my girlfriend. Yes, I want to sleep with her. No, I don't want to just be her friend. But I get her hesitation. Right before our eyes or not, she's a bit more grown up and responsible than me. I'm reckless with my emotions.

"Maybe next year I'll have no time to think about the questions to address. Am I the one to try to stop the fire?"

I've been out of the dating game for so long. I'm learning it all over again. There was a long period in my life where I went on dates just to get laid. If the girl annoyed me, I might still sleep with her, and then I'd never see her again, unless she was okay with just coming around for sex. If she didn't annoy me, well, we might talk for an hour and then have sex, and then repeat. When I lived in Texas, I lived in a city where I literally gave up on women because there just weren't any that I clicked with. And Corpus Christi is a small enough city to know who's out there, and whether or not they're what I'm looking for. They're not. The same thing applies to the job market, the entertainment options, and everything else there. It's not the place for me. I'm not saying I'm better than anyone there or that I'm too good for that city. I know a lot of great people there, who do great things and are very happy there. In fact, I know plenty of people there who are much happier there than I am here, or anywhere else I've been. And isn't that all that matters? And that's good. That city needs those people. Unfortunately, I am not one of them. Before those two years in Corpus Christi, I was in the Army, which is pretty much like going back to high school. I was very unhappy, and since I was unhappy, I made it my job to make others unhappy. I was an asshole. I was *The* asshole. Seriously. On more than one occasion I was told, "You know, I thought [so-and-so] was the biggest asshole in the barracks, but it's you." But to give credit where it's due, "so-and-so" was my best friend, and the title often went back and forth between us. Before that, I was back in Corpus Christi with minimal options, and the four years before that I was in a relationship. So, I forgot what it's like to date, to court, to woo, and to build a real foundation for a relationship. Yes, that first night I hung out with *The* Girl, I would've slept with her. But it would've been sex with a four-year history behind it.

I replied to her email and said that I wasn't expecting to get involved, but she should know that I respect her and our relationship enough that I would never just sleep with her and never speak to her again. She knew my history, so I considered that that could've been a reason for her hesitation. So, with the cards on the table, we kept hanging out. With other girls who didn't mean as much as this one, I just would've given up and tried to find someone easier. Not sexually easier, but more open to the possibility of getting involved. But this one is worth it. She makes me want to re-learn how to be *that* guy—the one who does everything right. Because if I do, and things work out, like I said, I will consider myself very lucky. So with our understanding that we weren't getting involved, she joined me at a small Two Door Cinema Club show in The Studio at Webster Hall a couple of weeks ago.

"I can tell just what you want. You don't want to be alone. You don't want to be alone."

I have a very strange history with Two Door Cinema Club. I definitely never want to see them alone. I discovered them in 2010 while researching Austin City Limits Festival bands before I was to cover the fest for a newspaper that I wrote for at the time. Brandon had flown down to Texas to go to the fest with me since I had an extra media pass, which meant unlimited free booze and minimal bag checks, which also meant that it was pretty easy to get whatever you wanted into the fest. And in this case, that included Adderall and cocaine. Two Door Cinema Club was at the top of my list of bands to catch that weekend. I don't remember which day they played, but I remember that a night of cocaine-fueled conversation with some other friends from Brandon's old music days led to waking up late and missing their set. I was bummed. Well, as bummed as one can get while under the influence of several different things while accompanied by his best friend. I moved on and we enjoyed the rest of the festival that day. When the fest ended that night, we found ourselves at a late night after party with more free booze. By that time, I was on the depressing side of a day of cocaine use and unlimited media-lounge whiskey. It didn't help that Brandon had met a girl and I had not. I guess it's kind of like when a rookie starts to rise above the old vet in a sport. Of course, I was always happy for my boy, but whenever Brandon succeeded before I did, I felt defeated. Which isn't necessarily fair. Brandon is better looking than me and he has his shit way more together than I do. On paper, Brandon should get girls more frequently than I do. But we're not talking about logical brain here, we're talking about a brain on Adderall, cocaine and at least 12 hours of drinking free whiskey and beer. (My how times have changed!) So, while Brandon was succeeding with a girl at this after party upstairs in the room where some band I didn't care about was playing, I wandered downstairs to a quiet room I found with no one in it. There I was, at a music festival after party...alone. I was only alone for a few minutes when two other guys walked in. They looked like the kind of guys who should feel the way I did. We started chatting, and I tried to hide my depression by talking about music. "Yeah, I'm just kinda bummed that I missed Two Door Cinema Club. They were the main band I wanted to see today." Then, before I had the chance to write an "in-case-of-suicide" note, one of them told me that Two Door Cinema Club was setting up upstairs. And everything was okay. Just like that. Like they say your sense of smell is tied to memories; music works that way with me. Two Door Cinema Club automatically makes me happy. So, watching them play an intimate show at Webster Hall, and having *The* Girl next to me the whole time was just perfection. But she and I weren't getting involved.

Since then, *The* Girl and I have hung out a few more times. She invited me to Philadelphia for a weekend. But we're not getting involved. She invited me to Atlanta, months from now. But we're not getting involved. She joined me at a Portishead concert because I told her if I went alone or took a dude, it might ruin the band for me. That was the date three nights ago. Me, *The* Girl, and Portishead. The last time I saw her, the night that ended in a kiss. Right now, it's looking like the plan backfired. Will my decision to take her to the show actually end up ruining Portishead for me anyway? But maybe a dark emotional confusion is exactly the feeling you're supposed to associate with Portishead, right?

So, there she was again, next to me—sometimes against me—radiating the feeling that everyone gets when listening to Portishead. After the concert, "our car" (like the concert, also part of my contest winnings) dropped her off, and she kissed me. Another great kiss. Another movie moment to me. But we're not getting involved. "You're a great date and a great kisser," she told me. But we're not getting involved.

"I can't say it's what you know. But you've known it the whole time. Yeah you've known it the whole time."

"Good Things" –
The Dangerous Summer

"My nerves start to feel so frayed. I'll try to turn things around but instead I'll say, 'Why do I feel so invisible? Good things will come my way.' I'll try to turn things around and wait 'til the day when I stop making big mistakes…"

When I moved into this hotel for the weekend it had only been two days since *The* Girl told me I was a great date and a great kisser, three days after my last Portishead concert…ever probably. I thought the tide was turning. Scratch that. There was no "thought" involved in that assumption. It was pure emotion. I felt the tide was turning. I hoped the tide was turning. I haven't heard from *The* Girl in two days and I still hope the tide is turning. Perhaps I should've started this chapter with "This is stupid." Well, it's not too late. This is stupid.

Yesterday was Friday. I knew better than to expect her to spend the weekend with me, and I really was determined to write. But after the amazing night we had together, I thought maybe the high hadn't faded with her like it hadn't yet with me. That never seems to be the case. So, the plan was to take her my spare hotel key and just say, "You can use this if you want, if not, no big deal." I knew I'd be risking setting us back, but like I said, I'm an emotional extremist. I'm also a grand gesture kind of guy. Hey, it works in the movies, and who doesn't want movie love? Sure, plenty of people don't believe in it, but I bet if they found it they wouldn't turn it down. Life is about experiences, and the best experiences always have some amount of risk attached to them. Those experiences with the most risk also have the most reward (so I keep telling myself). Unfortunately, they also come with the most pain if they don't work out. No ups without downs, remember? I just realized that my philosophy on life is the same as my philosophy on recreational drug use. Which reminds me, I think it's time for another Irish coffee and maybe another bit of Adderall.

I got to my room on Friday night. I had already started smoking because just the thought of taking that risk with her was riling up the anxiety. I popped some Xanax, drank some Johnnie Walker, and rather than popping open the MacBook and starting on my important writing, I grabbed a pen and a piece of Renaissance Hotel stationary that I intended to wrap my second room key in, and I wrote this:

"I will not be offended in the least if you decide not to use this. I just thought about it for a while and decided that I didn't want a party of strangers here, or to realize that I couldn't even get a party of strangers here, and that if I was going to share this awesome experience with anyone, it would have to be you. It has absolutely nothing to do with sex, because we're not getting involved. It just has everything to do with how much we enjoy each other's company and how the good times we've had so far only seem to be getting better. It has to do with you inviting me to Philly for a weekend, Atlanta in six months, and telling me I'm a good kisser. Trust me, I'm not reading anything into that (Because we're not getting involved), just as you shouldn't take this (or the flowers, or the kisses) to mean that I have any plans or ideas of where this is going. I just know that we're both attracted to each other and we both enjoy each other's company. Honestly, if Brandon were single, he'd probably be here, and we'd drink and have a good time…a sexless good time, which I know I can have with you. But I like where things are with you and me. So (here's that warning again), don't take this as anything crazy, I'm just the kind of person who likes to share great experiences with those who make them greater. Atlanta in six months will be better together. Concerts are better together. And this hotel would be too.

Like with the flowers, I'm not trying to convince you of anything or change your mind. Not getting involved is the smartest thing for both of us. But like I said after the first night we hung out, I respect our friendship enough to not screw it up. So all this is an invitation to come drink scotch, listen to good music, and stare at Times Square from 18 floors up. Actually, to stare at a giant P.Diddy billboard from 18 floors up. You're the only person who will know which room I'm in all weekend. If you show up, that's awesome. If not, no big deal. I seriously will not hold it against you because I'll take it as you doing what you think is best for our relationship. So, whenever we meet up again, this won't be a thing."

Yep. That's what I wrote. And I meant most of it. I would be okay with a "sexless good time" with her. I just can't charm her and make her fall in love with me if she's not around me. I folded over the stationary, slipped my spare key in the middle, and looked up the closest station where the 6 train stopped. Then I sought the liquid courage courtesy of Johnnie Walker, took some more Xanax to quell the frayed nerves, and some more Adderall so I wouldn't get tired from the Xanax. But none of it was working. It was ridiculous. I hadn't felt so anxious about a girl since probably fifth grade.

Kim Aguilar. I was just one of the many kids in our class who had a crush on her, which would wind up being the case for the next seven years of school. She became a cheerleader, she was smart, she was beautiful, and just as cliché as it was for a nerdy skater kid who played in a ska band to like her, she always dated the star football players. But in fifth grade, there were no cheerleaders. There were no football players. In fact, my best friend that year went on to be one of those great football players. Fifth grade was the last year we were all equals. The last year I could be delusional enough to think that I had a chance with Kim. And for a moment, it didn't seem delusional at all, but I suppose that's the true definition of the word. For a moment in fifth grade, she paid attention to me. I can't remember if it was because I was funny, which I always was to the highest extent of my years. Or maybe it was because I was slinging the candy my mom would buy us in bulk at Sam's Club, and always had an extra five-to-ten bucks on me, which is pretty baller for a fifth grader. I don't know. Maybe it was because I hung out with the alpha boys who eventually became the alpha males in high school, and I was just flying under the radar. But for that brief moment in fifth grade, she paid attention to ME. And I had hope. Even back then I thought I was beating some kind of system. Or I should say, even back then I realized there was a system, and even back then, I was stupid enough to believe I could beat it.

The details are hazy, after decades, but I recall the main points of the story. One day, we had a substitute teacher. At some point, she stepped out of the class, and a paper fight ensued. Spit wads were very popular back then, so I'm sure there were some Bic pen mouth canons involved too. I'm not going to say I started it, because I honestly don't remember. I was definitely the kind of kid who would start something like that, and the guilt I have from this story's ending, makes me believe I might've started it. Or maybe I just kept it going and escalated it when I saw Kim laughing and having fun, and wanted the credit for that. And of course, just like when this happens on any TV show, the substitute teacher walked back in and caught some of us paper-ball-handed. I was one, obviously, and star-student, future all-around-good-kid Kim was another. We got detention. (If this is an episode of *The Wonder Years*, that's purely coincidence. The ending should prove that. Winnie Cooper would never do this shit!).

I was used to detention. I was a growing adolescent boy being raised by a single mother with her hands full raising two boys and working minimum wage jobs. I might've already had quite the rap sheet for acting out (including eventually getting busted slinging candy like Lucas Sal y Limon and Tear Jerkers to other growing adolescent kids who needed their sugar fix and couldn't resist the rush of beating the rules to get it). But this was a first for Kim, and probably the last. However, it wasn't the detention that screwed it up for me. I have a vivid memory of her smiling in detention, too, so it couldn't have been that traumatizing. It's what happened after. When we all got out and walked to the front of the school to meet our disappointed and inconvenienced parents, my mom was in the first car in line, in our tan '76 Oldsmobile Cutlass, sometime around 1992. Nothing baller 'bout that. You'd think a young, enterprising entrepreneur like myself would come from better, I know. There was an obvious change the following days. I wasn't getting the same attention from Kim that I had before. I'd like to say I asked why, but it's fifth grade, so I'm sure I had one my friends ask one her friends, and this was the answer I got back: "Kim doesn't like you because your car's ugly and your mom's ugly." I'd also like to say I was filled with hate for her and no longer gave a shit whether she liked me or not, or whether she walked into oncoming traffic or not, because what a bitchy thing to say. But like asshole kids do, I definitely put a lot of blame on my mom for parking so close. Not that I ever thought my mom was ugly, before or after that comment. That car was definitely ugly as shit, with the color to match. Fuck that little girl for saying that. But growing up as poor as we did, I can't remember a time when I wasn't embarrassed by whatever car my mom drove, even when we had a '62 Corvair station wagon that I'd kill for now as an adult. But as a jr. high kid, coming to school in what essentially looks like a hearse, just made me wish I was dead.

I changed schools a few months after that day in detention. And towns. This was the beginning of a long life of being an outsider. I left that town for another small south Texas town 10 miles away, and I was gone for three years. When I returned in 8th grade, all of my past friends were well into their paths as athletes or marching band musicians, and the girls I liked were athletes and cheerleaders. I was a skater kid with bleached-blonde hair down to my shoulders, who was being kept alive by punk rock and being a class clown. So, just like in those cliché TV shows, I found new friends, and even though I stayed just as delusional about the same girls who were out of my league, I found new girls too.

So much for hazy details. Nearly two decades later and that fifth grade "romance" trauma still sticks with me too damn clearly. When *The* Girl inevitably disappoints me, will she haunt me well into my 50s?

I wanted to show her that there was nothing to worry about with me—that we should take advantage of the time we have together rather than miss out on something because of whatever fears we have of the future. But I also didn't want to blow it. Not with this one. Not with the one I've held on to for four years.

"'Til the day when I stop making big mistakes, and the clouds, they roll out of this whole damn state. I believe in a place and I wanna go. Honesty will leave me feeling livable...once I change."

I was "drunk enough to do it," as I wrote in a text message to Brandon. Sober enough to seek council, but not patient enough to wait for it. I left, and I walked to the nearest 6 train stop, which was only about five blocks away. The cigarette I smoked on the walk helped about as much as the couple swigs of scotch I took before I left. That is to say, not at all. But the whiskey and coke in this coke bottle roadie I brought should keep me from coming to my senses. I'm sure I blew my cover with the kind of swigs that no one would ever take from a Coke without booze in it. I was a mess. I wasn't even sure what I was getting in to. I think I accepted being such a mess because I didn't expect her to be home on a Friday night. That also meant that I didn't know what the hell I was doing (Adderall, Xanax, alcohol). If I got to her place, one of two things could happen: 1. She'd be home and I'd have to explain what I was doing, or 2. She wouldn't be home, and I'd have to wait for someone to come home, and hopefully let me into her building so I could slide the key under her door. Even though my blood and brain are just as poisoned now as I write this, as they were last night while it was all happening, I can see that there wasn't a lot of logic in my plan. But, when it comes to "love," since when has logic played a part?

I hadn't heard back from Brandon and it was time for me to go underground to catch the train that would lead me to my potentially harsh reality. This was going to happen. I'm sure my best friend would cheer me on. I'm sure he'd sit with anticipation to hear the glorious news that I made a grand gesture, it paid off and I got my New York-romantic ending (that he was a firm believer in too)! There's absolutely no possible way that I was thinking anything even close to that. This was a suicide mission and I knew it. And in this state of mind, with this many competing drugs in my system, quite possibly literally. She hadn't been responding to my texts. She told me she didn't want to get involved. I knew that I was walking into my certain emotional romantic death. I think I did it because it was exactly what I needed. You can't tell me I'm a great date and a good kisser and that you don't want to get involved. That's the kind of shit that gives a pathetic hopeless romantic like myself that little glimmer of hope. Tell me to fuck off. Tell me to grow up, get a life, get over it. Don't tell me good things and then do bad things. That just makes me think you just need a little bit of convincing. And I've always been pretty confident in my powers of persuasion. I'd like to say that I was marching towards the frontlines of her Upper East Side apartment with that confidence that I would convince her, but I wasn't. The scenario that went through my head—along with whatever chemicals the drugs and alcohol had pumped into it— could not even be compared to a firing squad. I knew that even if I got to her door and she answered, there's no way she would be as horrible as I would need her to be to convince me to give up. That's why I was there. I needed a nail on the coffin. I needed to say, "Look, I'm here." And I needed her to say, "Go away! Don't come back."

"Caught in the worst storm inside of me…and words start to feel misplaced. You can change what you want with your pen. I pray, as things start to feel much more possible, this time I'll know what to say."

When I came up from the train, 50 blocks away from where I boarded, I received the text from Brandon. Perfect timing. He suggested against it. I've "most likely had too much to drink." He was right, but for some reason that made me open the Coke bottle and take another deep swig—like it was straight Coke and I had just finished mowing the lawn on a south Texas summer day. "It will most likely not go the way you want it to." But he didn't know the way I wanted it to go. In my drunk, fucked-up mind, it was a win/win situation no matter what happened. She'd either be won over by the gesture, fall in love with me and take all that stupid "can't get involved" talk back, or she'd turn me down once and for all and I'd eventually move on. But maybe he's right. I know that if she's even there, if she answers the door when I knock, I know it's going to be the shittier of the options. And what if she doesn't answer the door? My imagination is going to run wild with the ideas of what she could be doing and with whom. As usual, Brandon, the smartest guy I know, was right. I took another swig and walked back downstairs, waited for a bit, debated going back up and just doing it, but eventually just got right back on a downtown 6 train.

The whole train ride the debate continued. In the movies, the guy doesn't change his mind like this. He RUNS to that apartment, bangs on the door, she answers, and they just kiss, right? Not in the good movies. I mean, one of the most iconic romantic scenes in (at least modern) cinema is John Cusack as Lloyd Dobler holding up the boombox playing Peter Gabriel's "In Your Eyes" for Diane Court in the movie *Say Anything*. Everyone remembers that. And it's remembered for its romance and parodied everywhere for the same reason. What people tend to forget, is that IT DIDN'T FUCKING WORK! Why not? Because even though Llyod Dobler was the best thing that ever happened to that uppity bitch, she didn't want to get involved. I'm perpetually Lloyd Dobler. In *Love Actually*, Andrew Lincoln's Mark puts together that sweet poster board power-point for Keira Knightley's Juliet, and, yes, it flatters her, and yes, she kisses him, but, IT DIDN'T FUCKING WORK!

The sad, pathetic, hopeless romantics go on being sad and pathetic. Sure, Lloyd and Diane Court eventually get together (no "spoiler alert" because that movie is 30 years old), after Lloyd asks Diane "are you here because you need someone, or because you need me?" After a long pause, and silence from Diane, sad, pathetic Lloyd says "forget it, I don't care." In the scene, the distraction of Diane showing up to Lloyd's kickboxing class gets him kicked in the face, leaving him with a bloody nose. So I guess he's just used to taking a beating. Goddamn you, cinema! Is this why I've accepted that it's just the way it has to go?

I sat on the train, drank some more whiskey and coke, popped my headphones in to drown out the thoughts and distract me from the happy couples that were heading out to enjoy their Friday night—as they should. And I'll just go back to my hotel, alone—as I should.

"I'll flee to a place that I wanna go. With a shift in the sound that is physical. Know I'll change."

I got off the train still not completely convinced I had made the right move. I hesitated. I turned around and listened to the automated announcer report the next stop. I watched the doors close and the train slowly pulling away. As it sped up, I reached my hand out, and I touched it. I touched the train. Now, that may not seem like that big of a deal. But for someone in the middle of a weekend-long bender with all kinds of chemicals running through his blood and all kinds of crazy thoughts running through his head, it's kind of a big deal. I remember that as a kid, I used to put my hands in the blades of the fan that was in my room. So maybe that's how big of a deal this was. What makes a kid put his hand in the blades of a moving fan? I dealt with some shit as a kid, but nothing really horrible. I wasn't beaten or molested or anything. I suppose the first time I ever really experienced depression was when my mom and dad went through their divorce in the early 90s. It wasn't so much the divorce that got me down back then, but it was more about my dad not really being around for us. At that young, was I able to come up with the concept of just wanting to feel anything other than the pain of your family falling apart and your father wanting nothing to do with you? Sure, teenagers cut themselves for that same reason, but I had to be like 10 years old when I was doing this. And, I don't know, maybe it's where I grew up, or how young I was, but I don't remember ever hearing about cutting, honestly, now that I think about it, until I knew females in the Army who were doing it. I do, however, remember one time I jumped off my bunk bed. Yeah, I was a stupid kid. Here I am, 20 years later and I'm sticking my hand out into a moving subway train. Maybe I'm a stupid adult too. Or just a depressed adult.

"Now that I've found some time, all the pain won't bother me. I've wanted to find what my head keeps filtering. That hole in my life, I just want it to die."

The fan blades didn't hurt back then, and touching a subway train as it increased in speed and disappeared from the station didn't hurt either. I needed it to though, and it didn't. I still felt what I was trying to not feel anymore. That's how bad it was. It was going to take a dismembered limb for me to stop thinking about *The* Girl. And, even then, after the initial shock, I'd just wonder how she'd respond if she knew what happened to me.

The train was gone. I thought about waiting for the next. A small part of me wanting to get on it and go back up 50 blocks, and another small part of me wanting to get in front of it. I had nowhere to be. I had no one to be with. I drank more. I considered breaking whatever stupid law says I can't smoke a cigarette in a subway station. But I just drank...more. I'd be lying if I said I've never thought of just jumping in front of a train and ending it all. Louis C.K has a bit about young single people being so insignificant that if they died, nobody would care. "Sure, your mom would cry," he says, but then explains that she would get over it and the world would not be different at all. I've been out of the house for over a decade—long enough that I don't really miss my mom or dad, and I'm sure that there are days when I never even enter their heads. And that's fine. That doesn't make me sad. That's life, isn't it? Isn't one of the goals of growing up to get to a place where your parents don't worry about you anymore? I don't miss my parents. I miss being loved. I miss feeling safe. Who knows when the last time that was? Did I even feel that way around family? I really can't remember the last time I felt loved or safe.

The reason touching the train is such a big deal to me, is because of what clicked in my head when I did it. As the subway sped up, things slowed down for me. I had enough time to think, what the hell are you doing? Is this it? So close. You're so close to...silence. So close to never having to wake up early for work again. Yeah, like my job was even close to what I cared about at that moment. *The* Girl is the only thing on my mind. It was almost midnight. The train was gone, and I was alone. I was alone except for a rat running around on the tracks below—the tracks I had considered throwing myself on. There were a few stragglers up and down the platform, and I wondered if they'd notice if I jumped down and just laid there. Would they try to stop me? How hard would they try? Just with words? Would anyone attempt to physically remove me? I stood on that subway platform for at least another five minutes after I got off the train, and those were the thoughts running through my head. So...close.

I wasn't feeling sorry for myself. I just wanted to be as carefree as that rat. Running on the tracks. Surviving. Barely, fucking surviving. Then a crazy guy started yelling at the tracks. I couldn't hear what he was saying because my music was too loud. Would I be yelling at the tracks if I didn't have music to drown out the shit in my head and actually had to confront my invisible demons? I mean, until this guy showed up, I was thinking about lying down in front of the next downtown 6. Now it looks like I gotta wait in line. Fuck, I'm the crazy guy. Until someone as crazy as that fucking guy shows up, I'm the crazy guy. More people have arrived on the landing. Waiting for a train for reasons that I'm sure are very different than the ones that crazy guy has or this crazy guy has. There's some concern in the eyes of the onlookers. I doubt they actually give a fuck about the crazy guy, they just don't want him to jump in front of their train and fuck up their night by delaying the mode of transportation that was going to take them to whatever happy place they were going to.

The next train arrived. He didn't jump in front of it, and neither did I.

"Your Heart is an Empty Room" – Death Cab For Cutie

"Burn it down 'til the embers smoke on the ground. Start new, when your heart is an empty room...with walls of the deepest blue."

Times Square is interesting. Well, I guess it has to be if millions of people visit it every year. But I'm sure it's a different kind of interesting to those people than it is to me right now. And, thanks to the Adderall, Xanax and scotch, it's probably a different kind of interesting to me right now that it would be at any other time. Although, I'm not sure there will ever be a time when I could be in Times Square without having Adderall, Xanax and alcohol running through my veins. How is it possible that we live in a world that hates commercials so much that we've invented a way to never have to watch them, yet this place is one of the most visited tourist attractions in the country? Being in Times Square is like being in that Willy Wonka invention that puts you in a TV, except you are only living in commercials. Was that a thing with Willy Wonka? Seems like it was. Maybe in the book? I don't know; I read the book in junior high, and I didn't see the Tim Burton version, which I guess was more like the book. The book had some freaky shit in it. At least freaky for a junior high kid. I'm pretty sure a kid gets eaten by squirrels in the book. Maybe I made that up too.

Times Square is like watching TV without TV shows. Now I'm not some anti-capitalist warrior who gives the least bit of shit about commercialism. I don't care that South by Southwest or other music festivals have become "too commercial." I don't judge my favorite bands for selling out. Hey, do what you have to do to be able to keep doing what you love. I just can't understand the people who buy into it. I'll let Rachael Ray feed me free BBQ at South by Southwest, and StubHub can give me all the free booze they want. I'm there to see the bands. But in Times Square, there's no benefit. It would be like going to South by Southwest to *look* at Rachael Ray or Perez Hilton—no free booze, no free food, no good music. Just expensive-ass hot dogs. I'm in one of the busiest places in the country—maybe the world—and it's all happening around me. I'm right in the middle of it.

"And all you see, is where else you could be when you're at home. And out on the street are so many possibilities to not be alone."

I had to get out of my room. Having anxiety is like having walls close in on you, even if there are no walls. And, the walls were closing in. I couldn't be back in that hotel room. For some stupid reason (Adderall, Xanax, scotch), I thought this would help. At least in my room, the walls that were closing in were tame—one color, not flashing, not yelling at me to buy whatever they're selling. For me, leaving my hotel room in Times Square to actually go out into Times Square is like being scared of clowns and going to a clown convention, and catching a ride there in a clown car, and then thinking maybe if I drop acid, this will be easier. I was standing outside Willy Wonka's Chocolate Factory, and now I'm in that fucking trippy tunnel he took everyone through. Not sure why that's the second Willy Wonka reference I've made. I haven't seen the movie in years. But that's how I feel now. I feel like I'm in the acid-trip Wonka tunnel, and the tourists that surround me are those squirrels that may or may not eat that kid in the book. And they're just waiting to attack. Does everyone understand anxiety a bit better now? At least *that* is the illness I'm dealing with now. Before I left my room, it was the depression too. It was loneliness. Is the change worth it? It seems like the circumstances don't matter. No matter where I go, I feel like I'm going to/want to die. Well, that took care of that. The loneliness is back. Now does everyone understand depression a bit better? I'm literally surrounded by at least thousands of people and I'm fucking lonelier than ever. I'll never understand why—and studies could be done on this—but I'll never understand how these people are happy here, and I'm not. It took a lot for me to get here, to this city, to this life. I should be happy, right? As I look around, I don't see one person who is alone. It's couples, it's families, it's tourist groups. It's people sharing the experience with someone else. Sure, maybe half of them hate it as much as I do, but they're sharing it with someone who is enjoying it.

I'm a pretty selfish person, except when it comes to love. I want to love with everything I have. When I think of *The* Girl—which apparently is a lot—I think I would happily walk through Times Square with her, if that's what she wanted. Although I'm pretty sure she would never want that, and that's why she's *The* Girl. But if she did, I'd do it. And I'd like to think I'd be, or at least I'd look as happy as the thousands of people around me. It's pushing midnight on a Saturday night, and I'm here, in Times Square, alone. Where is she? I want to imagine her home alone wishing that she was with me. She knows I'm at a hotel in Times Square, and, yes, that probably makes her less likely to want to be with me at this moment, since "we can't get involved." I want to imagine that she wants to love me with everything she has. I want to imagine, hope, wish, dream that she would want to love me so much that if I said, "Hey, let's go walk around the worst place on Earth," she would do it. For me. Of course, I'd never say that. But, if...if. It's always been about "if." Maybe someday it won't be anymore. That's what we're all hoping, right? Not here. Not in Times Square. Not in the place where I'm surrounded by people who aren't waiting for "if" anymore. Who knows how long they waited for their "if" to happen? Have I not waited long enough? It sure as hell feels like I've waited too damn long. It sure as hell doesn't feel like I'm any closer to all of those "ifs" finally happening. "If" she loved me. "If" she wanted to be with me. "If" I were in better shape. "If" my mom drove a nicer car. "If" I made more money. "If" I had my shit more together. "If" she's not the girl, then where the fuck is *The* Girl? "If" I screamed at the top of my lungs right now, would anyone notice with all these buildings screaming at the top of theirs?

I don't know when I started believing in *The* Girl. I don't know what made me believe that *The* Girl even exists. A friend once asked a group, "What was the first film that taught you something about love?" And even as obsessed as I am with pop culture, and how much I've dedicated myself to remembering the important pieces of it that have affected me, I couldn't think of it. *Moulin Rouge* and *High Fidelity* are big ones, but those definitely weren't the first. I can think of songs that influenced that thought at a very early age. Songs like Brian McKnight's "One Last Cry" and Bryan Adams's "(Everything I Do) I Do It For You." And music definitely taught me about love before film did, but there was still a first film. What was it? The first thing that comes to mind seems ridiculous to bring up, now, as an adult. But I can't help that it's what pops up. *The Great Outdoors*, with John Candy and Dan Akroyd. That film came out in 1988, I would've been six years old. Maybe it wasn't that exact year, but I remember the storyline about John Candy's "city boy" son falling for the pretty tourist-town local girl really resonating with me. But, damn, they don't even get to stay together in the end. Did I set myself up for a lifetime of failure by watching all the wrong TV shows and movies and listening to all the wrong music?

It's hard to remember a time when I didn't believe in what those things sold me. As I get older—every fucking day that I get older—it's harder to remember a time when I didn't believe in *The* Girl. That I didn't hope for *The* Girl. I remember one time I actually decided to talk to my dad about this stuff, he told me a story about a time when he had to come pick me up from school in my early elementary school days because I gave some girl flowers or something and she rejected me. I was so messed up by whatever it is that happened, that I went to the principal's office and just could not handle the rest of the day. So, dad had to come pick me up. And, apparently, it messed me up so much that I blocked it out and have absolutely no recollection of this incident whatsoever. And this had to be really early in elementary school, because dad wasn't really around to do that kind of dad thing after about third grade.

I do, however, remember a particular incident in fifth grade, after the Kim Aguilar detention incident. I had transferred to school number two of three that I was only at for part of that year. My mom had just moved us to a neighboring town to be closer to my dad. At least that's what I remember the story being. Now that I think about it, it was only about a three-mile difference, so I'm not sure how much sense that makes. We moved to a ranch in the middle of two school districts. So I went to one for a few months, then transferred to school three-of-three, in town three-of-three, to finish fifth grade, and stayed there through the first part of eighth. School number two was in in a town of about 600, so there was one fifth grade class—

probably less than 30 kids. I was still adjusting, but I remember noticing which girls were cute, but not thinking about making whatever moves you make in fifth grade like I had thought about it at my previous school where I was comfortable with my classmates. I remember we had some sort of dance around Christmas break time. Now, by "dance" I mean the 25 of us were in the room where we had music class, the lights were dimmed and the radio was turned on. A girl named Erica asked me to dance. Erica was definitely one of the cute girls, but I think I liked a girl named Lisa. Lisa had a twin brother who I had gotten in two "fights" with. And because I "won" these "fights," I think it hindered my chances with her. That didn't stop me from liking her. Now, I had heard that Erica had a thing for me—as you hear such things in fifth grade. But I had a one-track mind. So, when Erica asked me to dance, I had to say no. Here's the weird thing about this memory: I don't remember how Erica reacted. I only remember how I reacted. Erica quite possibly could not have cared less. Maybe my rejection didn't phase her one bit. She was a cute girl. Maybe she moved on to the next guy, and he wasn't an idiot, and he danced with her and they had the time of their lives. But me? I left the dance, walked to the hallway by the principal's office, sat down, and I cried. Even back then, I had this weird idea about love that—and I remember this clear as day—I thought I just broke this girl's heart. Like Kim had broken mine. I thought I ruined her life like the girl who hurt me so bad in third grade that my dad had to come pick me up from school. I felt like a monster. In fifth grade! That's how long I've been a fucking idiot about "love." Who remembers this shit so vividly? Fucking idiots about love, that's who.

I want to ask those people—the thousands of happy fucking people around me enjoying Times Square. What better place to get such a diverse sample from all over the world? Could the answer be right here in front of me with all of these smiling, picture-taking strangers? "Hey, couple walking hand-in-hand through Times Square, how did you know? How long did you wait? How sad were you and for how long?" Because for me, it's a lot and a long fucking time. What a perfectly sad way to ruin someone's night. But, hey, if it takes my drunk, pathetic, depressed ass to ruin your night in Times Square, well, then fuck you. Don't come back. I know it's the scotch talking. And the uppers...and downers. I'm not so naïve that I think that I'm the only one who has ever felt this way. I'm sure I'm not even the only person in the midst of these thousands that feels this way now. But, as I look around now, I can't spot the others. Can they spot me? If I can't see the other sad bastards around me, can they see me? Can the happy people see me? Or are they so lost in their bliss that a depressed, lovelorn lonely guy just gets overlooked like the homeless guy digging through the trashcan. Sure, you see him, but you don't skip a beat. The thought leaves your head as quickly as it entered. "It's a shame that such people exist, but, come on, honey, we're not going to let it ruin our night." That's me tonight. I'm the homeless guy digging through the trashcan. Don't mind me. Maybe you happy people worked hard for what you got. I've worked hard too. Jesus Christ, I have worked fucking hard to have what they have. But, sometimes, not all the times, but sometimes, you really do just get a bad hand dealt to you. I'm the guy at the table who has had bad hand after bad hand, but I've thrown my money in, my watch, the pink slip to my car—for some reason I keep playing, thinking it's eventually going to pay off.

"And all you see, is where else you could be when you're at home. And out on the street are so many possibilities to not be alone."

I don't hold it against them. Maybe they deserve their blissful happiness. I hope to have it one day, and I hope when (if) I do, no one will judge me for it. And when (if) that ever happens, who knows if I'll notice the sad lonely kid hoping that love exists? I hope I'll someday be so lost in love that I won't remember what it was like when I was just lost. Yes, I don't know why, but I still hope. Does that homeless guy digging through the trash still hope? What is he expecting to find in there? Will one more can or bottle to recycle change his life? Or maybe he's just digging for that one bite of someone's wasted food that will keep him alive until the next day when he can do it all again. Hell, I guess I've done that with women. I've dug through and found one that didn't change my life but just kept me alive 'til the next day. Is that what I'm doing? With the amount of Adderall, Xanax and alcohol in my blood right now, it's possible that I could not make it to the next day. Maybe that homeless guy doesn't know if he'll wake up tomorrow either. Are we both the same? We hope, we believe, but really, we're just fighting to live for another day. And for what? Is another day this sad, this lonely, worth living? What keeps us believing? Are we both just delusional? As he digs through trash, he sees people board the train, go to work, eat at restaurants. Does he think that if he lives just another few days, maybe he too will eventually get there? How is that any different than me waiting for *The* Girl while watching happy couples enjoy life together? How am I any different if I'm seeing what I want right in front of me, and I'm just sitting and hoping that if I make it another few days, I will eventually get there?

Have these people been where I am? Did they bounce back from digging through the trashcans and emerge to find the life they were hoping and dreaming of? Surely, some of them have been there. I guess if they're not giving up, I shouldn't. This is too much for me to handle without some more Xanax and scotch. I guess it's back to my cell.

"And all you see, is where else you could be when you're at home. And out on the street are so many possibilities to not be alone."

The Girl #2 – "Sorry About That" – Alkaline Trio

"It hasn't been that long, since we drank to the sunset until it was gone."

I wasn't always like this—this fucked-up. There was a brief moment of happiness when I first moved to New York City. It's the "greatest city in the world," right? And I had just left a place that I thought was one of the shittiest places in the world. I graduated from college after three tries in 10 years. I got an amazing job that wasn't a dream job, but definitely a steppingstone to one. I was living in a city that people who come from where I came from, and grew up the way I did, don't get to live. I was working at a place where those people don't usually get lucky enough to work. I didn't get lucky. I worked my ass off and it paid off. But, because I'm a fucked-up idiot obsessed with love, I still felt like something was missing.

Jaime was one of the first girls I met when I moved to New York. And, you know, I really didn't want her to come up because I hate letting her know that—even though some time has passed—she's still on my mind. Part of that is because we work together and I see her almost every day. And if I don't actually see her, I get an email from her or hear her name mentioned. Actually, that's the entire reason she's still on my mind. There are absolutely no feelings for her anymore except for some resentment, and I would hate for her to think anything more than that. But I suppose she is relevant to the story.

Other than the girl whose two-bedroom apartment I moved into, Jaime might be the first girl I met when I moved to this city. There were other girls at work who I already knew from my brief stint interning there six months earlier, but Jaime was the first new girl I met, and someone I interacted with on almost a daily basis. On my first day of work, she had to escort me to get my ID. I will give her this: she is beautiful. Smoking hot, actually. A little short, and kind of has a bitch face, but a pretty rocking body. If I kept track of the women I've slept with, she'd definitely be in the upper echelon of hotness. But while she was definitely one of the hottest, she's also one of the worst girls I've ever dated.

But when we met, I was vulnerable. Not in the hurt rebound sort of way, but in a new, naïve, doe-eyed-optimist sort of way. Fresh out of college and handed the ticket out of the town where I knew I would never meet the kind of girl I wanted to meet. I had just gotten the best job I've ever had, I had a sweet apartment in an awesome neighborhood and I was in the city where all my dreams were supposed to come true. The only thing missing was *The* Girl. We met because we had to, but I got to know her through hanging out with the girls at work who I knew from before. I was one of the few, if not only, single guys at work—at least in my department. Most of the people I work with closely were in the same age group, give or take five years. But most of them were also either married or in serious long-term relationships. So, I hung out with all the single girls. Not a bad place for a young, single, fairly attractive dude to be.

After a few weeks—and I mean a very few—Jaime instant messaged me an odd question. I mean, it could be seen as odd by some, but I knew exactly what it was. "Can I ask you something personal?" She asked. Already, that was a sign. If she already felt that comfortable with me, it was pretty safe to assume that something was going to happen here. Maybe most wouldn't jump to that conclusion, but I knew that was all the opening I needed. She had a boyfriend at the time, and they were having problems. And since, "my friends probably just tell me what I want to hear, and you're objective," she told me about the problems she was having and asked for my opinion about them. Another clear sign that something was bound to happen. I knew I had the upper hand (which never lasts long), since I didn't approach her as I'm sure most men do, because, you know, she's smoking hot. I didn't immediately jump at the opportunity to take advantage of the situation. I played it cool. I told her it was fine to talk to me about it because I would never consider dating somebody at work. Bullshit. But just in case she had any guard up with me, I wanted to knock that shit down.

The main problem, or so she said, was that her boyfriend never wanted to hang out with her. He always preferred hanging with "his boys." He also had no desire to leave their Long Island suburb and his bartending job for something bigger or better, and she did. As I got to know her better, under my Ted Mosby optimism and naiveté, I could not comprehend how a guy could not want to be around her all of the time. After a few months of dating her, I began to understand. I didn't know her boyfriend, and she was apparently unhappy with him, so there was nothing stopping me from making her the missing piece to my puzzle that was nearly complete. And for a while, she was.

For weeks, we chatted back and forth at work—all day, every day. We shared the same taste in music and we sent each other songs to listen to. I remember sending her a not-so-subtle message with the song "So Contagious" by Acceptance, in hopes of, but also knowing, that the lyrics wouldn't be lost on her. From the beginning:

"Oh no, this couldn't be more unexpected. And I can tell you I've been moving in so slow. Don't let it throw you off too far. 'Cause I'll be running right behind you."

(Boy, did that turn out to be too true.)

To the chorus:

"Could this be out of line? (Could this be out of line?)
To say you're the only one breaking me down like this."

I'm sure she took some of the songs as clear signs that I was interested in her too. I virtually spent every minute at work with her, and that wasn't enough. We took lunches together, we took more smoke breaks than probably either of us ever had before, just to have an excuse to talk and hang out. We danced around it for some time—not a lot, but some. I had only been at the job for about six weeks when we went on what we called a "fake date." It was perfect—except for the fact that she still had a boyfriend and I still had to play it cool. And I did. I was wearing a shirt I bought at The Juliana Theory's *Emotion is Dead* 10-year anniversary tour, and she complimented it. I never expect anyone to know who they are, and because I'm a music nerd and a fucked-up idiot about love and fate and all that shit, to me, this meant we were supposed to be together. But I played it cool.

Not long after that, we went out for drinks with some other coworkers. Jaime had to leave early for her commute back to Long Island, so I offered to walk her to the train. We had both had a few drinks, and when we got down into the subway station at the 1 line Houston stop, I kissed her.

"It hasn't been that long, since we drank to the sunset, until it was gone. And down with it went our pain and fear, as we slowly broke contact more and more, with every beer."

When the kiss ended, she slowly backed away. She didn't seem like she wanted to, but more like she had to. She still had a boyfriend, and if she didn't at least act like she felt guilty, then she ran the risk of me thinking she was a horrible person. I told her it would never happen again, so she wouldn't think I was a horrible person. Of course, hoping I'd be wrong. Nothing changed. Things were the same at work. We talked about her shitty boyfriend. We flirted. We ate lunches and smoked cigarettes. I spent more time with her than almost any actual girlfriend I'd ever had. Then came another coworker's birthday party.

It was a Friday in August. I had only been in New York and at my new job for two months, and this is where we found ourselves. After drinking through the evening in Williamsburg, we got to the birthday party at another bar near Prospect Heights and drank some more. She bitched about her boyfriend to everyone, I flirted with another girl friend of one of my coworkers, and she got jealous and let me know. Another great sign. She hinted that she was not looking forward to the long late-night train ride back to Long Island. And if that's not a sign, I don't know what is. The bar was only a few blocks from my apartment, so I asked her to come home with me. It didn't take much convincing. No convincing at all, really. We strolled through Brooklyn and I told her that I would keep my word and not kiss her. "But," I said, "if you want to kiss me, you can." She must have wanted to. She must have been wanting to, because

I was stopped in my tracks with her lips against mine almost at the exact second I finished that sentence. She kissed me a few times on that walk. She played the "I feel guilty" act again. And then she said, "I can't keep kissing you because then if we're ever together, you won't trust me." I didn't know it at that moment, but I'd soon find out that she was right. She came home with me, we made out a little bit, and then went to sleep.

"And we passed out each other's arms, both admitting we'd never felt better, never felt so warm. But awoke in each other's eyes, without wearing a stitch of clothing, we were both deeply in disguise."

The next morning, there was no guilt. There were no regrets—at least none were expressed. We both knew that it felt right. We both knew that we were great together. She knew that two years had been long enough to waste on a guy who didn't see her the way I did. I walked her to Atlantic Terminal to catch the LIRR, and kissed her goodbye.

"Maybe I just set aside the fact that you were broken hearted in my own special selfish way. And if I hadn't set aside the fact that you were broken hearted, hell knows where your heart would be today. Maybe with me."

After that night, things moved fast. Like, crazy fast. And neither of us worried about it. I was obviously lost in the bliss of what I thought was the feeling of being complete for the first time in my life—job, city, *The* Girl. Maybe she was just feeling good about having someone paying some genuine attention to her. That month, August, two months after I moved here, she and I joined a gym together—like a fucking couple, and we went, often. The timeline's a little hazy, but she did eventually break up with her boyfriend soon after that. He didn't take it well. He went from being mean to her to being apologetic and then back to mean. She reported every detail to me. She was also never really sure about what she wanted to do. She and I would go out after work on Fridays and sometimes she'd go back to Long Island and sometimes she'd come home with me. Once she had broken up with the guy, she had no problem spending the night with me or having sex. I was so lost in how perfect I thought everything was that I didn't see that there was no possible way that could be true.

"Maybe I just set aside the fact that you were broken hearted in my own special selfish way. And if I hadn't set aside the fact that you were broken hearted, hell knows where your heart would be today. Maybe with me."

One night, we went out after work, around the place where we went on our fake date. We had a couple of drinks, and then we made out in an alley like a couple of high school kids whose parents dropped them off at the mall. We didn't care who walked by, hands were under clothes and faces were devouring each other. But she had to catch a train back. So we walked to the station. I don't remember what was said first, but her response was "I love you." To me. She said that to me, after something like two months of dating. Sure, as I tell this story, I see red flag after red flag, but, like I said, I thought she was all I was missing. I didn't say it back immediately. We talked about it for about 10 minutes and she said with a little fear in her voice, "Maybe I do love you." And because I'm a fucked-up idiot about love, I said the exact same thing back. "Maybe I love you too."

Within a month of that, she decided it was time to move to the city. She started looking for apartments in my neighborhood. Red flag, I know. And then one night, she texted me, "Let's just be crazy and move in together." This was about three months in. There's another one. Did I run? No. I told her that I knew she was going to play it off as a joke, but we both knew that it could work. We never talked about it again. I went apartment hunting with her——for one-bedrooms, not really discussing if they were just for her or for us. We continued to date and we continued to sleep together. At work, we continued to take our smoke breaks and would occasionally sneak in a short makeout sessions whenever we could—as we walked around the block smoking, anytime we ended up in an elevator alone, anytime we ended up in a stairwell alone. One night, during an after-hours in-office Halloween party, she and I found our way up to an empty floor and got ourselves a little action. And things were going alright—until they just weren't. She started cancelling plans. Suddenly she could never make solid plans. Maybe she was getting spooked by the speed we were going, but I was just following her lead. We'd still make out in elevators and stairwells at work, but all of a sudden it was like she was doing the testing of the waters that you do before you say "I love you" and talk about moving in together—only she was doing it after those things had already fucking happened.

"It seems like it's been so long since we kissed through the darkness, until it was dawn. Up with it came our pain and fear that we'd already lost each other. We both knew that the end was near."

October was the beginning of the end, and the end wasn't far behind that. We had a work event to attend and we had decided to attend as each other's dates. By this time, my mind wasn't as fucked-up as it was a month earlier. But this night was going to be what got us back on track—or so I thought, and with good reason. She met me at my place, where she would be spending the night, and we showed up to the event together. We both had work responsibilities to attend to, but we met up at the after party. We managed to sneak away to make out a little, and everything seemed fine. Then she gave her number to three guys in front of me—within a fucking hour or so. So, yeah, my night was pretty much ruined. Once the night was over, of course she came home with me, what other choice did she have? That was the original plan anyway, but Long Island is nearly impossible to get to that late at night. If I were a true asshole, that wouldn't have mattered to me. No. Not an asshole. I would've been justified in kicking her to the curb. We got into bed, I tried to kiss her, she said, "Can we just go to sleep?" I didn't answer. I got out of bed, got some extra blankets, threw them on the couch, and told her she could sleep there. It wasn't "put out or get out," it was, "Fuck you. You gave your number to three dudes and you won't even kiss me goodnight? Yeah, you're not sleeping in my bed." It was me trying to convince myself that I had some self-respect.

It didn't take her long to apologize. Within minutes, she texted from the other room and asked if she could come back. A text! Couldn't even be bothered to get up. I ignored her. I don't think she was used to getting kicked out of a guy's bed and she needed to get me back under her thumb. I held strong that night, but not much longer after that. Things never were the same after that night, but we did talk a little bit like they might possibly be again. My birthday was a couple weeks later. She swore she'd be there. Promised. All night I waited. I had a great group of friends celebrating with me, but the only thing that was on my mind was where she could possibly be and who she could be with. She never showed. Hell of a way for a guy to turn 30.

There's a Taylor Swift song called "The Moment I Knew" about exactly that (see, I listen to everything). She stares at the door during her birthday party, waiting for a person who promised to be there.

"Christmas lights glisten. I've got my eye on the door, just waiting for you to walk in. But the time is ticking. People ask me how I've been, as I comb back through my memory, how you said you'd be here. You said you'd be here."

She's all dressed up, but the person never shows. She tries to hide the hurt from her friends but they see through it, as I'm sure my friends did. And that was the moment she knew. She doesn't say what she knew. That the person was an asshole? A selfish piece of shit? My person never showed, I got wasted, and when I went home, I had sex with the *actual* first new girl I met in New York: my roommate. Sure, it was pretty great, really great actually—I had been attracted to her since I met her, but had never planned or intended on sleeping with her. But it happened, and it happened one or two more times after that, but always in what seemed to be a mutually utilitarian sort of way. Welcome to New York, right? That night, my birthday, with my roommate, my mind was definitely not in it. That's not how Taylor Swift's night ended, or at least not according to the song. In fact, the Taylor Swift song ends with the guy calling to apologize for not showing up. Jaime did eventually call me to do the same, but, like Taylor, I already knew.

Within a couple weeks of my mid-November birthday, Jaime was openly dating a new guy at work. More openly than she and I had ever been. By our company Christmas party, she and he looked the way she and I used to look behind closed doors, which led me to believe that she had started seeing him before she stopped seeing me. Just like she had started seeing me before she had stopped seeing her ex-boyfriend. He may have even been one of the three guys she gave her number to at that work event where she was my date. The only one I remember was a D-list celebrity who played the least attractive recurring character (not even a supporting actor) on a basic cable show that revolved around average-to-unattractive guys who were really into fantasy football. I tried not to pay attention that night, tried to play it cool like I wasn't bothered by it, so I can't say for sure whether or not her new guy was one of them. Before the year was over, she moved into *his* neighborhood, in a completely different borough—maybe two months after we talked about moving in together. There was also a good six months that I had to see the two of them walk into the gym that she and I had signed up for together. She was right, I never really did trust her. There's a difference between being delusional and trusting someone. I was definitely the former. She couldn't leave her boyfriend without having me as a fallback, and when she found a new fallback, she had no problem tossing me just like the last guy. I never held it against her new guy—whom I dealt with pretty closely at work. He didn't know me at the time and she's a hot girl. He was just doing what any dude would've done. He was just doing exactly what I did a few months before. But I do hold it against her.

I've dated some shitty chicks in my day, but she's definitely top 10, no, top five. In her defense, she was young—24 to be exact. Yes, a part of me says I shouldn't be defending her, but we all did some shitty things when we were young. Plenty of people do shitty things when they're not-so-young. When I was her age, I hurt friends and ruined relationships because I was a young, stupid selfish kid and I did things that young, stupid, selfish kids do. This doesn't change her rank on the "shittiest girls I ever dated" list, but I chalk it up to her being a young, stupid, selfish kid. It's partially my fault. I should've known better. I knew she was young, still lived with her parents even though she wasn't *that* young. She wasn't capable of being single, which meant she wasn't comfortable with herself. She didn't like her job and constantly felt like she should be something better than a secretary, but never really did anything to achieve that. As my friends have told me, and I've found to be 100% true, I was blinded by her hotness. She was never nice to me. She just spewed horrible things and bitched about everyone including just random strangers who had absolutely nothing to do with her life. She was just horrible. Hot, sure, but horrible. So, the deep depression I fell into for the months after that is not entirely her fault. I should've known better.

"Maybe I just set aside the fact that you were broken hearted in my own special selfish way. And if I hadn't set aside the fact that you were broken hearted, hell knows where your heart would be today. Maybe with me. Maybe with me. Maybe with me.

"Duality" – Bayside

"Some days, I get crazed. I don't know why. It's so irrelevant. I'll take deep breaths and keep control, go on."

It takes longer for Ambien to kick in after you've popped Adderall to make sure the Xanax doesn't knock you out when you're on a roll bitching about a hot girl at work who stomped on your heart. Did I mention she was hot? I need a cigarette.

Well, fuck, that didn't help. I'm not sure what's going on with my body now. Technically it's Sunday. My mind is saying—no, my mind is screaming—"Go to sleep, motherfucker!" And, believe me, I'd love to. At least I think I'd love to. I'd love to be a normal, healthy person who sleeps when he's supposed to and can get out of bed without the help of Adderall. But that's what depression is. Sure, I've listed a few drugs (over and over) and none of them have been antidepressants, but that's because I've never taken an antidepressant that makes me less depressed. I've only taken antidepressants that make it harder for me to ejaculate. And in instances like these—when I'm all alone—if masturbating has no end result, what could be more depressing than that?

"I've tried brave, and you've tried to save. I'm proud to keep it bottled up. I think I'm past my prime and lost my mind and I'm torn."

So, I accept being depressed. I want to feel. If I can't feel, what the fuck am I supposed to write about. I just need to feel, go to work (Adderall), chill out if it gets too crazy (Xanax), and go to sleep when necessary (Ambien). Except, in this case, the Ambien ain't workin'. Maybe that's okay. It's only (technically) Sunday morning, so I don't necessarily need sleep. I've got another day and night in this hotel, might as well make the most of it. I sure as hell am not going to make the most of it by lying in that king size cloud alone. I tried. Fuck it. It's almost the actual morning, might as well have another coffee. That should go well with the sleeping pill if it ever decides to kick in.

"No telling what tomorrow holds."

I thought memories of Jaime—my bitterness, her hotness— were going to keep me awake, hence the Ambien. It's been a long time since I've thought about her like that. I cut her out of my life as much as I could when all that shit happened. At first, it took quite a bit of Xanax—every day at work. I saw her every Tuesday at our boss's weekly meeting. I turned in my timesheet to her every Friday. And on top of that, there were the occasional run-ins with her and the new guy at the gym. But she and I were a long time ago, so it stopped hurting as much. Then eventually it just didn't hurt at all. I stopped seeing her as a girl I loved who broke my heart, and I was finally able to start seeing her as just a shitty person who was just looking out for herself. And, you know what, when I was her age, in my early-20s, I was the exact same way. That's when I left the "best relationship I've ever been in" because I wasn't ready for it. And I don't want to hear any of this shit about karma. That's not why this happens to me. Plenty of shitty people never experience shitty things, and plenty of good people never experience good things. Maybe you mostly reap what you sew, you get what you pay for, but most of the time things just happen. The only "belief" that we can all agree on is that everything could be and should be a learning experience. Now, whether you choose to learn from it or not, well, that's your call I suppose. I'd like to think maybe someday she'll look back on us and, sure, maybe she won't wish she was with me, but hopefully she'll at least realize she handled things poorly. It's also very likely that she'll just stay horrible and never feel bad. Plenty of people take that route, I suppose.

I popped the Ambien, boarded the most comfortable bed I've ever slept in, and when my head hit that pillow, it wasn't Jaime that was flying through my head. It was *The* Girl. Friday and Saturday night had come and gone and I hadn't heard from her. Was it bothering her as much as it's bothering me? Well, definitely not *as* much. She has her shit a bit more together than I do, so I'm sure she's not abusing prescriptions (I actually prefer the phrase "exploiting prescriptions"), binge drinking scotch and chain smoking. Is she at least wondering what I'm up to? Am I at least keeping her awake? The reason I have a Ambien prescription in the first place is because most nights I can't shut my brain off (obviously). Thoughts of what I want to do with my life and questions about what I'm doing with my life, just constantly swoop around in there. If I let them linger long enough, I get overwhelmed. Maybe I should be doing something else. Can I really achieve the things I dream of achieving? Not tonight. Tonight, the only future or present on my mind is the one involving *The* Girl. I want to call her. I want to text her. That's nothing new. Those urges never leave me. Maybe this is a test. Everything that's led up to this weekend has shown that she and I are pretty great together. She's even said as much. But then "we can't get involved," or "I just need some space."

"Who let, who let this feeling die, when all I did was try? Who let you let this feeling die? I can't get you out of my head, my head."

I don't want to get her out of my head. *She* is why I'm writing. *She* is one reason I kept working so hard to get up to New York. *She* is really the first girl who made me think, yeah, I'm ready, I could settle down. *She* makes me try, *she* makes me want to be the best at everything I do, so *she* will never think I'm not good enough for her. Because to me, *she* is the best I've ever known.

"You're the flame that burns me, so I know that I'm still alive."

And now Friday and Saturday nights have come and gone, and *she* could be in some other guy's arms for all I know. The bars of Manhattan are coming to a close, and *she* could be on her way home from a bar where *she* gave her number to three dudes. My texts have gone to her phone unanswered. That is what kept me up when my head hit that pillow. *She* is stronger than Ambien, and that shit is strong. I don't know if it's finally kicking in or if my body is just finally giving up. More Irish coffee.

What am I supposed to do? Just give up? Based on experience, the answer is probably simple. Isn't there some saying about how anything worth having doesn't come easily? This has been four years in the making. I'm not the only one who felt that first kiss. There are few people who have been in my life that long. So there has to be a reason, right?

"Some say, it's all fate, but I say we control our lives. And if my destiny should out best me then that's fine."

I'm obviously not in control of any of this. Maybe if I were smarter I could be. If I were smarter I would've seen the red flags with Jaime. If I were smarter, I would've seen Meghan for what she was: one amazing night in New York. I wouldn't have fallen in love with either of them. If I were smarter, I wouldn't be writing a book about a girl who "can't get involved." Just saying that makes me need some Xanax. I'll be asleep (or dead) in no time. If I'm being honest, which, obviously I am, I did see those things. I'm a smart guy. But when it comes to "love," say it with me: "Fucked. Up. Idiot." Even though I let myself be delusional about those girls, it was always just hope. Never confidence.

"The truth is doubts are all I've got to call mine."

I fight for it. I believe in it. I convince myself that I can make it happen. I can make it work. I just have to do or say the right thing, and in the blink of an eye everything will be as perfect as I know I deserve them to be—if I just make the right move.

"Is there anybody out there? Is anybody calling? What if what I say is really wrong? I'm not in control. I think I'm out of control."

I've seen the movies. I've read the books. I know what to say. I know what to do. When *The* Girl is with me, she lets me know I'm doing everything right. I did everything right with Meghan. With Jaime, I followed *her* lead. And she led me right off a fucking cliff. How do I keep ending up in the same place? One minute, everything's perfect. The next second, the complete opposite. It was three or four days ago when *The* Girl told me I was a great date and a great kisser, not to mention the perfect dates we had before that. Now: unanswered texts and an imagination running wild. She knows I'm a fucking writer. She knows I have a vivid imagination.

"Who let, who let this feeling die, when all I did was try? Who let you let this feeling die? I can't get you out of my head, my head."

I don't want to get her out of my head. I haven't given up hope. *The* Girl is worth it. Sure, it might take some work. Sure, she's put me in a state where my body feels like it's about to power down, maybe for good. Feels like the Ambien's kicking in. Or maybe I'm just dying. Welcome to anxiety. This is what *The* Girl does to me. But aren't those the ones worth working for?

"You're the flame that burns me, so I know that I'm still alive."

I'm definitely still alive for now, and as long as I am, or at least until she gives her number to three dudes in front of me, I'm going to live for her. I'm going to work for her because she's worth it. When I think of the kind of girl I deserve, the kind of girl who would actually make me happy and actually make me feel genuinely complete, it's her. I hope it's the Ambien I'm feeling and not, you know, death.

"Never Feel Alone" –
The Dangerous Summer

"I drank the weekend to the ground, and you're in my arms. I kept my feelings to myself, and you weren't wearing much at all."

Can you guess which part of that line is true? It's Sunday morning. I'm running out of time. I upped my Adderall dosage. I'm running out of time. I told myself that this weekend I would write, and I haven't done enough of it. I'm running out of time. I started writing when I was 18. It's over a decade later and I've written enough album reviews and concert reviews to fill a couple of books. But I haven't written enough of anything to fill a book that anyone would want to read. I'm running out of time. I've upped my Adderall dosage and I'm finally starting to get it. I never was much of a drug user or abuser, but then, I was never much of a writer. I'm finally starting to get it. I've upped my Adderall dosage (can you tell?), and I've smoked more cigarettes this weekend than I have in at least the last few months. There's nicotine in my blood, speed, maybe some left over Xanax, and plenty of alcohol. I'm not sure how much blood there actually is left in the mix. A pot of coffee is brewing so I can keep going. Okay, a pot of coffee is brewing, now, because I want to drink scotch and I'm too scared to drink it straight because I'm already shaking and my heart is speeding up. You'd think the three hours of sleep that I got would've rejuvenated me—given me the energy to wake up well-rested and ready to attack the task at hand without requiring any extra boost. Yeah, I guess nobody would think that. What the fuck, Ambien? You let me down. Normally that shit knocks me out and I wake up feeling well-rested. It's the only sleep aide I've taken that has worked that way. For a short while I took a drug called trazadone. That one was fun. I had the most vivid dreams on it—so vivid that I would wake up and write them down. I wrote pages and pages—dreams of an ex-girlfriend I hadn't thought about in at least seven years, dreams about Britney Spears, who had already gone through her crazy phase but was not yet in her return-to-hot phase, and one night I woke up from a dream right as a wolf pounced at me, only to go back to sleep and return to the world where I was being stalked by that same goddamn wolf. Pages and pages I wrote. Man, where's trazadone when you need it? Maybe I shouldn't blame Ambien. She's been good to me over the years. Tonight, and this whole weekend, she's had a tough opponent with all the Adderall in my veins. When I woke up this morning, I didn't give myself time to realize that I probably didn't need any more Adderall. I just woke up, saw the bottle and thought if I took some I would immediately get to work. Well, I got to work. My heart is racing and I'm looking around a room that hasn't had anyone but me in it all weekend like I'm expecting to see someone else. My hands are shaking and I keep looking at my phone that she hasn't texted in days like I'm expecting that to change all of a sudden. And I finally get it.

"A feeling's just a feeling 'til you let it get the best of who you are. Then sleep gets harder and I need more of you."

I get why so many writers or other creative people took to the poison. Or at least I think I do. I feel like I'm going to die. I honestly feel like at any second my fast-beating heart is just going to burst. I feel like this could be my last day on earth. And that makes me write. I think I'm running out of time, and I could very well be. So I write. Hot damn! Finally, justification for the pills and booze and the loneliness and the torture. Finally, some motivation.

There was a bar a few blocks away from the first apartment I lived in here in New York. It's New York, there's a bar a few blocks away from every apartment. That particular apartment was only a few blocks away from Columbia University, so there are actually a lot of bars nearby—a lot of college bars. When I first moved here, I explored my neighborhood and thought that that was a good thing. Only a few blocks away from cute, smart college girls? But I was also a few blocks away from good-looking, smart college dudes with money. There was a time in my life when I was really great with women. Maybe I still am. I think I just got tired of it. I got tired of the pointlessness. I got cynical. At one point, when I lived in L.A., I dated women who were way out of my league. When I returned to Corpus Christi with the confidence that L.A. instilled, the girls I got who were out of my league in the looks department were not anywhere near my league in the everything-else department. So, I had a lot of sex—a lot of meaningless sex—with beautiful girls. I stopped caring. I stopped believing. Those who knew me didn't understand it. I mean, they understood why I would want to fuck hot girls. They just didn't understand why those hot girls would want to fuck me. Maybe if I had stepped back and taken a look at my life back then I wouldn't have understood it either. But I was high on something else back then. My mind was clouded, but in some sort of blissful cloudiness of girls, and definitely booze, and sometimes cocaine. Back then, I didn't feel like I was running out of time, so I wasted it. It really fucked me up. Now when I go to a bar and see beautiful women, I play the scenario out in my head.

"She's cute. I could say the right things and take her home, and we'll have great sex—or at least sex. But then we won't have anything in common. Or then she'll say something stupid. Not stupid for her, because she's just a 21-year-old college chick. What does she know about life? But stupid for me."

And I would hate myself if I wasted any more time on *those* women. I'd convince myself that that is my life. Doomed. Like tonight.

I'm at this fucked-up point in my life—and at too late in life—where I'm interesting and fun enough for the younger women to like me because they have a good time with me, but then they realize that I should have my shit more together. So, I leave them before they reach that point. It's the same case with women who are my age or older. I'm fun, interesting, and exciting—a loose cannon, a wild card—because I'm not as straight-laced as the guys they're used to. They, too, eventually realize that I'm not a safe bet. And when they've had their fun, they leave too—unless I beat them to it. I usually beat them all to it.

One of the things I love about New York is that you can walk anywhere, and everywhere is interesting. There's so much history in this city, and I don't just mean the old stuff. One night when I was leaving *The* Girl's place—depressed, drunk—I decided to walk home. The Upper East Side might sound like at some point it's just right across the street from the Upper West Side, but really there's a giant forest in between called Central Park. I knew that, but I decided that rather than wait for a late night 6 train to take me to whichever train that would take me to a C train, or take a cab, I'd walk. A few blocks away from her apartment, before the dark forest that I will never cut through again, there is a firehouse. I can't remember if I was drunk on either whiskey or wine that night—it was always one or the other with us, and I always drank more

119

because I wanted her to drink more because when she drank more she liked me more—but I was drunk on something. I'm sure some sad bastard music was playing in my ears, because sad bastard music was always playing in my ears. Maybe I didn't feel like I was going to die like I do tonight, but I felt like I wanted to die. Four years, at that point, I'd been hoping for this girl, and it wasn't happening. She knows me. She knows the great things about me. We have things in common and she doesn't say the stupid things. She was the one who things were supposed to make sense with. And nothing was making sense.

"So lay down on the couch and let me show you why I need you more than all the boys on your street."

It was probably a Sunday night. She's a smart, beautiful, cool girl—she always had better things to do on Friday and Saturday nights. Like Lloyd Dobler, I didn't care. I wanted to be with her whenever she'd let me. It was after midnight, but I don't recall how far after. The streets were quiet. I've always found it insane that, late at night, parts of Manhattan, the "city that never sleeps," can be as quiet and empty as they are in post-apocalyptic movies. I had to pass the south end of Harlem to get to my place, which was more on the west-edge-of-Harlem than Upper West Side. I didn't mind. I've stayed in Harlem a few times in the past and never had any trouble. But this time, before I hit the park, I walked by this firehouse, and outside that firehouse there was a poster with black-and-white photos of all the New York firefighters from that house who died on 9/11. It was fucking sad. But, again, it was sad on kind of a selfish level. Some of those men meant something to wives and children, I thought. Those who didn't, they still mean something to the millions of strangers who live in our country. I didn't even mean something to a fucking girl I had held on to for four years. I could keep walking to the next bar that might be half-filled with more people I don't mean shit to. On that day, those men ran up a burning fucking building to serve the purpose that they felt like was theirs. Maybe some of them felt like they were going to die. Maybe some of them knew they were going to die. Maybe some of them did it because they wanted to die as heroes.

I feel like I'm going to die today—right now, any minute. And that is the only thing that makes me do what I believe is my purpose. And what have I written about? Drinking, doing drugs, being depressed, stupid girls. I want to die a hero. Don't we all? I mean, we at least want someone to miss us when we die. Don't we all want our lives and deaths to affect somebody? I've known this girl for four years, and she let me walk through Harlem at 2 a.m. drunk? I could die today. I'm not anyone's hero. I need some fucking Xanax.

"So here's the thing with my head, I'm unstable. I'm feeling honesty come out, when really I'm just gone."

I'm not crazy. Okay, maybe I am crazy. But feeling the way I do about *The* Girl, thinking the things I think about her, is not crazy. I'm not delusional. Some might call me crazy to think there was an immediate connection the night we met, but that's how I believe these things happen. Even today, after all the shit, I still want to believe that that's how these things happen. She and I have since talked about that night, and I've found out that I was not wrong.

I met *The* Girl in Chicago. The night I'm remembering may not be the first time I met her, but it was the first time I actually spent time with her. I had visited Chicago three or four times that year because the girl who I was on and off with for four years had been going to grad school there. On this particular visit, the last of them, I was no longer "with" that girl, but we had decided to stay friends. It must've been around December because, on this particular visit, she and her classmates were celebrating their graduation from one of the most prestigious journalism graduate programs in the country. I was there to help celebrate, and that meant that I would be going out around Chicago with her and her program's small graduating class, which was comprised mostly of females. *The* Girl was one of those females. I remember we started off at someone's apartment on—is it Lakeshore Drive? Anyway, it was a nice apartment right by the lake with six-to-ten girls and, I think, one guy who was married, and I was the fairly attractive guy who just flew in from L.A. I had met most of them in passing in my previous visits, so they all knew me as their classmate's boyfriend. On this particular visit, if it hadn't been made known beforehand that I was no longer her boyfriend, it was probably made obvious pretty quickly that night. We hit some bars and then we ended up at karaoke—and we've established what that means to me. I don't remember how many songs I sang, but I never only sing one. The only song I remember singing is Marvin Gaye's "Let's Get It On." I was in Chicago, *High Fidelity* is my favorite movie (yes, I've read the book, too, but I've seen the movie probably over 100 times, so it's easier for me to reference that, you judgmental snob), so I took a risk. And, yes, I tried to sing it as close to Jack Black's version from the movie. Now, I don't know if you've ever tried to sing "Let's Get It On" at karaoke or anywhere for that matter, but it's not an easy song. I did already know that. My ex-girlfriend wasn't going to help me out with it, so I enlisted *The* Girl. She didn't take much convincing. She took the stage next to me—wearing a Rolling Stones t-shirt and a maroon denim skirt that was a littler longer than I liked (it's been four years and I can still picture her like it was yesterday)—and we gave it our best shot. I think we were all drunk enough by this point to just have fun with it and not care how good it sounded. It probably sucked, otherwise I would remember killing that song in front of a bunch of girls. But that, unfortunately, is not a memory I have.

"So now's the part where I get closer to you."

Singing that song is one of the two things I remember from that night. The other thing happened at some bar where everyone ended up dancing. I was dancing with my ex for a while—as a good guy should—and then I think she went to the bathroom or something, and then I was dancing with *The* Girl—like an asshole. My ex is a smart girl. I'm sure she saw it at the karaoke bar, maybe even earlier. Now we were all drunk, and I recall some grinding between *The* Girl and me. Yes, that's what I wanted. She was what I wanted. It wasn't just because she was cute. Throughout the night, I got to know her a little. She was fun. She was funny. She didn't seem to care what anyone thought about her.

("A feeling's just a feeling 'til you let it get the best of who you are.")

And I was apparently too drunk to care what my ex thought or how she felt that night. Sober me wouldn't have been such an asshole to a girl I did still genuinely care about very much.

"Am I wrong, or is this really what you want to happen? When all I want to do is have this, I'm not strong enough to breathe."

Jesus, this story is bumming me out. It's like my brain and my heart are parts of two different bodies—and I don't at all mean that in a romantic sense. I mean it in a physical, I-still-feel-like-I'm-going-to-die sense. My heart is still racing, but my brain is being a fucking downer. Oh, that's right, all weekend I've been loading uppers and downers into my system like coal into a fucking old-timey steam engine. Who needs a refill of scotch?

"'Cause I'm caught in every single word and I know that you are something else. Yeah, I've reached my point."

I know, a drunken night of bar hopping does not a Chicago fairy tale make. That was just the first night. Isn't that how Harry Met Sally? I know. It's not. Let me present exhibit B. There used to be this great music festival in New York City called the College Music Journal Music Marathon. For a whole week in the fall, over a thousand bands from all over the world come to the city and play in something like 70 different venues. As a music nerd, how could I miss such an event? As a music journalist, I definitely couldn't. One year, some friends of mine from Texas flew in to partake in the festivities. One of those friends was my best friend in college. He was completely up-to-date about *The* Girl. I invited her out on one of the nights for a couple of reasons: 1. I knew I would be able to show her the time of her life, 2. I wanted her to meet my friends because, in my head, they were going to be her friends, too, when we ended up living happily ever after, and 3. One of my favorite bands, The Front Bottoms, was playing and I wanted her to love them as much as I did, thus realizing that she and I were meant to be together. Believe it or not, the night kind of did go just as planned. Kind of.

First of all, she missed the band I wanted her to see. But that was okay. By this point, I was already drunk from going to shows all day with my friends and drinking free booze from whatever corporate sponsor provided it. Before *The* Girl arrived, my two friends and I met two girls—cousins, one from Pennsylvania, the other from Jersey. Hey, two girls and three guys, I didn't care. Why would I, when *The* Girl was on her way? The two girls had been doing exactly what we had been doing, so they were good and buzzed too. When they found out that we had Adderall on us, well, they weren't going anywhere. They thought we were cool, we thought they were cool. Then, the cuter of the two, snatched a tablet of Adderall, crushed it up and snorted it. Can't remember if she was the one from PA or Jersey, but I can guess. This was going to be a good night.

The Girl caught up with us, and we ended up at some event sponsored by a car company, where the Cold War Kids were playing. Big corporate sponsor usually means free booze, and this time was no different. We spent some time there and *The* Girl caught up to us real quick. Can you say, "meant to be"? At this point, it's probably the early hours of the morning, and we made our way to the lower east side to catch Peelander Z—a band I've always described as "if the Ramones were also secretly The Power Rangers and Japanese." I've seen them at least three times and they're always amazing. I don't know if she just said it for me, but *The* Girl said she liked them too. I felt like this was the night we needed. It was finally happening. It's funny how your brain picks and chooses what to remember. I don't remember where the next bar was. I don't remember how we got there or why we went there. I do remember that the bar was dead and my Texas friends gave all the girls two-step lessons. Oh yeah, and my best friend from college fucked the cuter girl in the dirty-ass bathroom downstairs. Mission accomplished! I wanted my friends to come visit and have a real New York adventure, and they did. They flew out the next morning. It's only now that I realize that, for my college buddy, maybe that night was his "Megan." We never really talked about it and we've since lost touch. I know both of those guys stayed in touch with both of those girls. I talked to the less-cute one a few times after that night because we had the same birthday and talked about celebrating together, but it was just talk. Maybe my buddy romanticizes that night like I did with Meghan, maybe not. He really wasn't ever the hopeless romantic that I was/am.

("So here's the thing with my head, I'm unstable.")

There was almost a decade age difference between me and that friend, so maybe we just grew up on different movies. Maybe when I listened to music, I listened to it differently. I'm not saying I'm better or he's worse. Hey, who's about to die alone in a hotel room from upping and downing through a lonely weekend of trying to play "artist"? It's funny how your brain picks and chooses what to remember.

"Well I plan to do my very best to let you know that you're in my head."

This memory hurts so much that I wish I could forget it. I wish I remembered how and why we got to that last bar instead of remembering this stupid memory. But it's this memory that is the exhibit B that proves that I'm not delusional—at least not in this situation. After the two-step lessons, after my buddy banged the cuter cousin in the bathroom, *The* Girl and I went outside. I feel like there was some cigarette smoking, but I could be wrong. This part, however, is unfortunately clear as fucking day. *The* Girl told me what a good time she had. She told me that she always has a good time with me. She told me that she wanted to be with me, and she didn't stop there. She said that she knew WE were going to have a good life together, and she didn't stop there. She said that she wanted to be by my side to cheer me on as I write. She talked about this life we would have, filled with listening to music together and going to shows together. And you know how I know she meant it? She also said, "and sometimes I won't go to a show with you, but that doesn't matter." In about five minutes, she planned our life out, and she made it sound realistic. It was all I ever wanted to hear her say and she was saying it. In real life. My New York romance was happening. At that moment, all the other girls didn't matter. At that moment, it was like *The* Girl was saying, "Congratulations, you made it." All that hard work and heartbreak was finally paying off. At that moment, I thought, *this* is why I never gave up on love.

"Am I wrong, or is this really what you want to happen? 'Cause all I wanna do is have this, I'm not strong enough to stand. 'Cause I've been pushed around before. I felt the burn from every inch of my heart. But it's worth it to never feel alone."

The Girl and I went back to her place that night. For the first time, my Texas friends had to find their way to my apartment on their own, but they didn't mind. They knew exactly what *The* Girl meant to me. They knew what that moment meant to me. That night, they saw a New York movie happen in real life too. And, to them, it was exactly like watching a movie. They got to see it end on that happy moment before the couple embarks on whatever happens next. For me and *The* Girl, what happened next is also a memory I wish I didn't have. We had what was probably the worst sex of both of our lives. And I don't just mean me. I haven't held back yet, why would I start now? I don't know if it was the booze, the Adderall, or the pressure of everything that led to that point, but neither of our parts were working the way they were supposed to be. That's the prettiest way to paint that picture. We tried. We both wanted it. And we worked it out a little, but we were the opposite of R. Kelly's "Bump 'N Grind." Our minds were telling us yes, but our bodies, our bodies were telling us fuck no. Fortunately, we were both drunk enough to just pass out without having to deal with the awkwardness then, and we were friends enough to laugh about it later (since it was mutual). Unfortunately, she decided that we weren't going to get involved before we ever got a chance to redeem ourselves.

"Am I wrong, or is this really what you want to happen? 'Cause all I wanna do is have this, I'm not strong enough to stand."

The Girl #3 – "Miserable at Best" – Mayday Parade

"...don't cry. I know you're trying your hardest. And the hardest part is letting go of the nights we shared."

I've never done heroin. I don't think I even know anyone who has. Scratch that. I do have a friend who has told me that he used it for a while, but, as far as I know, I didn't know him while he was using. He's still alive and well today back in Texas, and he's a pretty good musician and a very funny comedian. We've done coke together, and occasionally I'd share my Adderall and Xanax with him when I was back there. That's what friends are for, right? I really have no real-life experience with that drug though. At the time when I was hanging out with this guy, he was popping the occasional hydrocodone, which he said had similar effects to heroin. I've messed around a little bit with that in the past—less than five times—and I don't remember it really being anything to get excited about. Hence, the minimal usage.

I bring up heroin because I think I want some now, and it's not the first time I've thought that. I've actually thought that a lot. Like with many things in my life, my only knowledge of it comes from what I've seen on TV and in movies. In TV shows and movies, when people use heroin it looks like they just completely shut down. They look relaxed. They look like they completely forget about whatever the thing was that made them stick a needle in their arm in the first place. But the bad side of that drug (that I've seen in TV shows and movies) is what has kept me from trying it out. Like I said before, I've always had pretty good control over my vices, but I'm not sure if my writer's ego is strong enough to resist the ability to never feel this fucking pain again. If I could shut it off—I mean the pain—sure, I wouldn't hurt anymore, and I definitely wouldn't write anymore. I probably wouldn't do anything but just be that blanked out body sitting on the floor, back against the wall not feeling anything. That sounds very easy to get addicted to. If I did decide to ever try it out someday—which I figure would've happened by now if it was ever going to—I'm pretty sure I'd snort it and not shoot it. I don't have any issues with needles or anything. That just seems like a little too much effort. But, who knows, I guess sometimes you just reach that point.

Thinking of *The* Girl all weekend makes me wish I could just stop feeling. Thinking of her has made me think of the other *The* Girls who made me wish that, and it just builds and fucking builds. I just washed down another Adderall with some more Johnnie Walker. If it's a fucking upper, why don't I feel "up"?

It took me a minute to remember how and where I first met Amber—*The* Girl #3. We didn't hang out that many times. Definitely less than 10, probably closer to five. So, I traced back our steps. I thought of the last time I saw her and worked my way back until it finally came to me. The first night I met her was at a friend's birthday party. This friend was female, and, yes, I was interested in being more than friends with her. That's why I was there. So, when Amber showed up, like the other pretty girls there, I didn't really pay attention to her. It probably also had something to do with her giant boyfriend who showed up with her. I can honestly say that the thought didn't even cross my mind on that night. I was so oblivious to her then, that the next time I saw her, I thought it was the first time meeting her.

Amber is beautiful. And she's like naturally beautiful. She never looked like she tried very hard to look pretty. She just looked pretty, always.

"But compared to your eyes, nothing shines quite as bright. And when we look to the sky, it's not mine but I want it, so..."

That second time I met her for the first time, she met up with me and that birthday friend that I was interested in for trivia night at Pete's Candy Store in Williamsburg. Now, bar trivia nights are just like karaoke nights for me—whatever I may lack in the looks department, or in physical prowess, or financial stability, I more than make up for in my abundance of the often-useless knowledge upon which the bar trivia industry is built. Let the seduction begin, or so I thought. Pete's Candy Store trivia is no joke. I still managed to contribute more than my fair share, but nothing too impressive. Yes, I was technically there with Amber's friend, who I was interested in, but Amber's friend had made it clear that she was not interested in anything serious with me. I know just about everything I've written in this book makes me sound like a pretty pathetic hopeless romantic—and for a while, I was that with her friend, but I never just sat and waited like a puppy dog. Had she changed her mind, I would've rushed to her lap like that puppy dog when he hears the bag of doggy treats being opened, but I knew that wasn't happening anytime soon. I was dating, exploring my options and keeping my eyes and mind open to other possibilities. I wish I could say that even on that second night with Amber, I immediately considered her a possibility, but that wasn't the case.

First of all, I did think she was a bit out of my league in the looks department, but that's never stopped me before. The fact that she had a giant boyfriend who could and would crush me if he had to, also did not deter me, because I had completely forgotten that I met either of them. What made me hesitate on this particular night was the guy that showed up with her this time. He was a stud. I've never been attracted to a man enough to question my sexuality, but I have absolutely no problem admitting when a dude is a good-looking dude. This guy could've been a male model, in my opinion, but like for an H&M or some other hipstery chain—not like ripped abs, shirtless Abercrombie male model. When they joined us, they sat very close together. Sure, Pete's Candy Store gets pretty crowded on trivia night, so this was necessary, but they looked all too comfortable about it. Now, boyfriends aren't necessarily a deal breaker for me, obviously, but that's really only in the case that "the juice is worth the squeeze," as Emile Hirsch so eloquently put it in the underrated comedy *Girl Next Door*. If a girl is going to cheat on her boyfriend, then she probably shouldn't be with him in the first place. That being said, I would only overlook that detail if I thought the girl was really someone I could have something good with. At this point, I wasn't thinking that about Amber...yet. Plus, the guy she showed up with was probably one of the nicest guys I've ever met. I'm not an asshole, at least not all the time, and definitely not as much as I used to be. There was that period in my life where I made some pretty stupid and very selfish decisions just to get laid. I like to think I've grown out of that. Maybe I learned from the consequences that came from those decisions, or maybe I've just gotten that all out of my system. I can honestly say that for most of that night I didn't even think of the possibility of going out with Amber.

We played our trivia rounds—taking full advantage of the $5 shot-and-a-beer special that Pete's had to offer. She never played the girl card, that so many do, when we all went whiskey shot for whiskey shot together and chased them down with PBRs. She was a woman after my own heart. Trivia ended, but the night didn't. We all hung out for a while longer, and I got to know her a little better. That's when some good things were found out, and unfortunately, some bad things. She was a writer—for a living. I don't know, maybe I have a lot of weaknesses when it comes to women, but a girl who can write is definitely at the top of that list. She wrote bar reviews, which, to me, meant that she liked alcohol enough to carve out a career that revolved around it. I love a lady I can drink with. She also came to New York from Texas, and I'm not sure how we got on the topic, but we grew up listening to the same kind of music: punk, ska, and even the embarrassing Christian versions of those genres. More good news: the super nice, extremely good-looking dude with her was her brother! The bad news: she had a boyfriend. The worse news: in something like two months, she had the option to move to France with him.

When I look back on the story of Amber and remember the boyfriend detail, I always only remember that he was a huge guy who could crush me, and that he had some kind of job that paid very well—the two things that were working against me. That night, and every other time we hung out, when she mentioned this opportunity to move to France, she never sounded certain about it. I know she hadn't been with the guy for very long—I don't think it had even been a year, but I could be wrong about that—and that was an issue. When she talked about France, she talked about it like it was just a great opportunity for her to leave a job that she wasn't incredibly happy with, live in a beautiful romantic country with a guy that she at least liked, and she would not have to work and she could focus more on writing. I totally understood that. Hell, I'd do the same thing. So, while I was getting more and more interested in this girl with every word she said, I knew exactly what I was up against. Challenge accepted! I don't know why it was accepted. I obviously do not have a good track record with these challenges. Something in this fucked-up brain makes me think that if a girl isn't a challenge, then she's not worth it.

She never stayed on the subject of France for very long, and you could tell it was because of how uncertain she was about it. We eventually landed back on music, and it just so happened that the following week, I was going to a reunion show for Five Iron Frenzy—a Christian ska band that we both loved when we were growing up. I never expected to meet anyone as excited about that show as I was, but she was, and she wanted to go with me. I looked it up on my calendar, and she and I spent a few minutes looking at all the other concerts I had planned on going to between that night and the day she planned to leave to France. She was excited about most of them, and said she wanted to go with me to some of them. I was down for the count. That night, the second time I met Amber for the first time, I knew there was no way I could let her go to France.

"You're all that I hoped to find in every single way. And everything I could give is everything you couldn't take."

We met up about an hour-or-so before the concert to pregame at a bar near the venue. That's usually how it goes for me before I go to shows, since New York music venues tend to have pretty ridiculous prices for drinks. Yet, I still end up paying those prices when I'm there and drinking as much as I would have even if I hadn't pregamed. But Amber and I definitely had a good buzz going before the show, and on the walk to the venue, she pulled out a one-hitter, and we smoked some weed. I didn't see any reason not to. I was going to a concert with a pretty girl. I wanted to have the best time I could with her, because, for all I knew, she was going to be gone soon. Plus, I'd be lying if I said I didn't consider the irony of smoking weed on the way to watch a Christian band that I grew up listening to. I dedicated a big part of my developmental years to that world, missing out on the drinks, drugs and sex of high school and my first years of college, only to be dealt disappointment after disappointment from God and his followers. Plenty of years had passed since I had broken up with God, so when I say I considered the irony, that's really all it was. I was over the period of being spiteful towards God, or maybe I just knew how stupid and pointless that was. In fact, I don't think I ever had a spiteful period. This was my indifference period. At the concert, we drank more, we both sang every word to almost every song, and she led me to the front of the crowd.

"You're all that I hoped to find in every single way. And everything I could give is everything you couldn't take."

It was a perfect night, so far, and my fucked-up, pathetic, hopeless romantic brain that believes in New York movies was starting to think something was happening, and I wasn't about to do anything to make my brain think anything different. The end of the concert was only the beginning of the night. She said her office wasn't too far away from the venue, and she suggested that we go there and take advantage of their office bar. I'm pretty sure she also said something about smoking and drinking on a rooftop there. That all sounded pretty romantic for a night out amongst two friends, but of course, that was exactly what I wanted. She was the kind of girl I moved to this city to find. I didn't want to be her friend. I think we smoked some more weed on the way to her office, because, the next detail I remember seems like something that would only happen if we were high.

When we got to her office, she put her key in the door and just could not get it open. This was something she had done on a hundred weekday mornings when she showed up first, but on this night, she just couldn't figure it out. We both tried for what felt like forever, which is another reason I think we were high. It was probably just like 5 minutes, but you know how those weed minutes can feel like hours. Eventually we gave up and decided to head back to Brooklyn. She lived in Williamsburg and I lived a little further in Bushwick, so we hopped on the same subway. There was going to be a day really soon that I was probably going to have to say goodbye to her for good, and thankfully, we had an excuse to make the night last a little longer. There were things that I did want to say, but I knew better. I wanted to say, "Look how awesome we are together." I wanted to say, "This could be us." I wanted to say, "I know France sounds great, but *we* can go someday." I wanted to ask her to stay.

"Because the words were never easier for me to say, or her to second guess. But I guess I can live without you, but without you I'll be miserable at best."

We got on the L train and headed for Williamsburg. Those New York romance gods that I so naively believe in, well, that night they decided to remind me that they exist. The train was semi-crowded—enough that I had to practically hold her in my arms for us to get in there. She put her head on my chest, and moved in closer than she needed to be. A couple minutes passed before she kissed me. She. Kissed. Me. We kissed a couple of times on that train ride. I finally got to be one of those people who I fucking hate seeing on the train. We kissed, and when we kissed, it felt like I wasn't the only one who had spent all night hoping for it. When we got to her stop, I offered to walk her home. I can honestly say that I really did just want to make sure she made it there alright. Yes, I wanted to sleep with her, but I was going to be perfectly fine if, when we got there, she kissed me goodnight, and then I made my way to my place. When we got to her place, she invited me in. We kept kissing, and this time we were kissing like we were in an empty apartment, not a crowded train. We found our way to her bed and her shirt found its way off. As I started working on her pants, the guilt hit— her, not me. We stopped. Just like I could honestly say that I would've been fine not even coming into her apartment, I can honestly say that I was fine not going any further. I really liked Amber. I wanted something real with her, and I still believed that it was possible. There were still a couple months before she was supposed to leave. If we got that far the first time we hung out together, maybe something real wouldn't be too far off. I didn't want to blow our chances. It was a great night, and I left it at that and headed home.

The next time I saw her was at another Pete's Candy Store trivia night. We started making that our weekly routine. We played, we drank, I smoked cigarettes, she hit her one-hitter, and when the night was over I tried to kiss her. "That's not gonna happen," she said. I was disappointed, but I wasn't discouraged. I really did want to respect the fact that she had a boyfriend. My main concern wasn't fucking her. My main concern was spending time with her so she could see how great we could be together. I was running out of time to convince her to not leave for him, but I needed her to feel comfortable around me so I could do that.

"Let's not pretend like you're alone tonight. I know he's there. You're

probably hanging out and making eyes, while across the room he stares. I bet he gets the nerve to walk the floor and ask my girl to dance. She'll say yes."

We had a couple more trivia nights, but they were nothing more than hanging out and getting more comfortable with each other. Then, I had a name night at a bar by my office in Manhattan. Name night is one of the greatest inventions ever, and every drinking establishment should do it. It works like this: If it's your name night, you drink for free. Brilliant! Normally when this happens, I invite as many friends to join me as possible so I don't have to be a sad lonely drunk. This time, I only invited Amber, and she came. It was a Saturday night and the bar was dead. That was actually pretty normal for this place because it's in a part of TriBeCa that's made up mostly of office buildings and is only busy during the week. She walked in and I almost fell to the ground. She looked hotter than I had ever seen her look. Like I said, she always looked effortlessly hot, but tonight she looked like she took some time and she looked like a fucking model. I'm pretty sure it was the first time I had seen her in a skirt, and it was a really tight skirt, maybe leather? I wanted to throw her down on the pool table and just have my way with her. Instead, I racked them up and we played a couple games and drank. It was only a matter of weeks, now, before she was due to depart, and she was still talking about how uncertain she was about leaving. Not only that, but also about how uncertain she was about the guy. Music to my ears. It was like she was asking to be convinced.

We drank more, played pool a little more, and grabbed a table. When we were together, it always seemed like we both felt like the time we had was never enough. We were supposed to meet up with our mutual friends in a different part of town, so we left that bar and started walking. I asked her if she wanted to see my office since we were so close, and she said yes. We got up to my floor, I gave her a quick tour, showed her my desk, and we started making out. She led me a little further than last time, and led my hand up her skirt. It felt premeditated—like she dressed for the occasion. But we didn't have a lot of time, and it didn't go as far as I think we both would've liked. Maybe the guilt hit her again, or maybe, you know, the beige cubicle under white fluorescents wasn't the most romantic setting for a couple's first time. Would've been pretty fucking hot though. I don't know. If that was the case, she didn't mention it this time. I played it cool since we were still going out, and I thought maybe things would escalate throughout the night. When we got to the bar where our friends were, we split up to find them. I found them, but lost her. It was Saturday night in a part of town that was the opposite of the dead one we just left. I was bummed out. When I got to work the following Monday, I noticed that, at some point when she and I were in the office, she wrote a short note on a notepad on top of my desk. It had a big heart drawn in green highlighter and read:

"Best. Night. Ever." Followed by her initials.

I think I saw her maybe one more time before she left to France, but that night at my office was the last night we had alone together.

"You're all that I hoped I'd find, in every single way. And everything I could give is everything you couldn't take. Cause nothing feels like home. You're a thousand miles away, and the hardest part of living is just taking breaths to stay."

I think a part of me just needed her to choose me. I didn't look at it as a competition that I needed to win. It had nothing to do with me-against-her-boyfriend. I was trying to display how great I could be for her, like I have with every other girl I had really fallen for. I just needed one of them to finally realize it and accept it. If Amber had been that one, I know I would've been really happy. It would be a win for me, but not in the competition against the other guy. It would be a win in this fucking marathon that I've been running by myself for what seems like forever. It would prove that this New York romance dream I've been chasing wasn't just a product of my fucked-up mind. Maybe I think that if I find it, it will be all the evidence I need to prove that my mind was never fucked-up in the first place. "I'm not crazy, I swear! Look! Proof!"

"Because I know I'm good for something I just haven't found it yet. But I need it."

I just needed it to be over. She was the finish line that I knew existed, but never seemed to come into site. If I couldn't win Amber over, it meant that I was going to have to keep running. And who knows how much longer I'd have to keep running? A lot of time has passed since Amber, and I'm still fucking running. I don't know how much longer I can keep it up.

"Because the words were never easier for me to say, or her to second guess. But I guess I can live without you, but without you I'll be miserable at best."

I'm not miserable without Amber. I'm miserable without *The* Girl, and at that point Amber was *The* Girl. At one of our trivia nights I gave her a copy of *Love in the Time of Cholera*. I read that book for the first time because John Cusack's character in *High*

140

Fidelity says it's one of his favorite books, and, well, it's also the book that Kate Beckinsale's character writes her phone number in in the movie *Serendipity*. She tells John Cusack's character in that movie that she will give it to a used bookstore the next day, and if the book comes across his path someday, well then they're meant to be together. What can I say, I'm a kid of the 80s and 90s; I love John Cusack. If he points out a book to me, I'm going to read it. However, I read *Love in the Time of Cholera* the second time because it's about a sad, pathetic, hopeless romantic who falls in love with a woman—and she falls in love with him but is forced to marry someone else—and he spends the next 50 years of his life just hoping and waiting for his chance to be with her. He never loves another woman, although he has sex with like 600. I gave her a copy of *that* book. I was clearly trying to send a message. I guess I thought she could still be convinced, or maybe she'd read it while in France and come back. Yes, I am that stupid. I believe in the love that so many books and movies are written about. No matter how bad the journey to find it hurts, why settle for less?

A few months after Amber moved to France, she came back to visit New York. She stayed with friends who lived on my block, so it was easy for us to cross paths, and to see each other without having to make an excuse. One night, when her other friends weren't home from work yet, she stopped by and we caught up. It was great to see her, and while I wasn't still hanging on to her by then, I did still remember how great we were, and a small part of me still believed that maybe someday down the line we'd get another shot. Of course, every night that she was in town I hoped that maybe we would at least hook up to get that out of our systems. I sat in my apartment doing whatever it was that I had to do, and I just hoped for a knock on my door. Then it came. It really happened. She knocked on my door. See why I believe in this shit?

I opened the door. The amount of hope that I had for it to be her kept me from looking or feeling surprised. Had it been anyone else, I probably couldn't have hidden my disappointment. I invited her in, but she had to decline. She had to pack for her flight back the next morning. I knew that was coming, which is what made it more confusing seeing her standing at my door. I really thought this was it. It was finally going to happen for us. And it, being with *The Girl*, was finally going to happen for me. Surely, I thought, she was coming to me so I could give her a reason to stay. No.

She remembered that, the night we hung out, I mentioned that I had Xanax. She asked if I could spare some. Of course, I could. Of course, I did. I handed it over and...she kissed me. She fucking kissed me. And not just a goodbye-and-thanks-for-the-drugs peck. It was like we had crossed into a parallel universe—one in which she had never left. Then she went back to our friend's apartment where she spent the rest of that night. And I never saw her again.

"But I guess I can live without you, but without you I'll be miserable at best."

"Kill" – Jimmy Eat World

"Well you're just across the street. Looks a mile to my feet. I wanna go to you. Funny how I'm nervous still. I've always been the easy kill. Guess I always will."

I broke. I bought a pack of cigarettes. I paid $13 for the same pack that would cost me around $5 back home in Texas. I've been in New York for a few years now, and I still use the word "home" when I refer to Texas. If I did the math (which we've already established that I don't do), it would probably equal up to at least half my life that I've lived outside of Texas. Yet, that is where I still refer to as home. I still don't love this city like I was so sure I would. Like the women who have come and gone through my life, I've wanted to love it. I've tried with everything I have to love it, but she just doesn't seem to want to love me back. I moved to New York with the naïve enthusiasm that a child has when he goes to Disneyland for the first time. I was excited. My life was about to change and it would never be the same. But when I got to Disneyland, it was super crowded, everyone was pissed, and all that was there to greet me was overpriced hot dogs, giant pretzels, pretty buildings and gift shops. But like that naïve little child might think, I tell myself that surely it will be better the next time. Every morning I wake up in this city and I think that, and I'm almost always wrong. Some days it's better, but it's never what Disneyland is supposed to be.

I bought a pack of cigarettes. I want to say it's mainly because I was out of cigarettes, but I'm not a smoker, I can be okay being out of cigarettes. I bought a pack of cigarettes because I needed to get out this hotel room. The fear was catching up with me. It is catching up with me. Fuck that, it's caught up with me. The extra Adderall that I took on top of the extra Adderall I took earlier today might have something to do with that. I keep noticing new levels of how fast my heart can race without exploding. I've discovered new levels of how much my hands can shake while still be able to type words on a keyboard. I'm finding out how much one can feel like they're dying without actually dying. I'm only in this hotel room for one more night. With every day it seems to be getting smaller and smaller. I had to get out. I suppose if I did die in this room at least my body would be found tomorrow, sprawled out or maybe just sitting in this chair that I've spent most of my time in this weekend. While everyone I know was probably out having fun in the company of friends, I've been in a shitty desk chair in front of a computer, feeling like I'm on death's doorstep ringing the doorbell with anxiety that wants to look for an unlocked window and just break the fuck in. Turns out, writing about loneliness doesn't make you any less lonely. Writing about being fucked-up in the head doesn't make you any less fucked-up in the head. Some poor housekeeper, who would probably remind me of my mom, would find me limp and lifeless, in front of closed pill bottles and an open laptop, with an unfinished book next to a finished bottle of Johnnie Walker. Who would care? I'm nobody. I don't have other books that people have loved. No one would say, "Oh, no, he had one more in him and now we'll never know how it ends." Or maybe this is how it ends. But no one would care enough to finish it for me. I have to be the one who finishes it. But shit's getting dark. How is it that I think about *The* Girl with every waking second, in every single one of the tens-of-thousands of words that I've written, and she can't even fucking send me one goddamn text message? Has one thought of me even crossed her mind this weekend? It's been almost a week since we kissed. Not one fucking text. But maybe it's for the best. If she had been more receptive this weekend—or receptive at all—there's no way I would've gotten this far.

"Could it be that everything goes 'round by chance. Or is there one way that it was always meant to be. You kill me, you always know the perfect thing to say. I know what I should do, but I just can't walk away."

Shit's getting dark, but that seems to be the only way I can write. Every normal day of my life I deal with hurt, but it's just emotional hurt. That's fucking Major Depressive Disorder for ya. Hurtful thoughts, all the time. But this weekend, I'm also a physical mess. I'm tired of feeling this way. Depression and anxiety. I know how much I have to do to feel like I actually accomplished something this weekend. If I don't feel like I accomplished something this weekend, then all this fucking pain—emotional and physical—wasn't worth it, right? So rather than add some Xanax to the mix, I thought that maybe a cigarette was all I needed. That was just part of it. I've been in this hotel room for days, alone, writing about how long I've been alone. I didn't want to be alone anymore—not that I ever wanted that in the first place.

I bought a pack of cigarettes, found the quietest side street I could find, sat on the first ledge I came to, lit one up, and put this Jimmy Eat World song on repeat. Back to *Futures*. I'm not a smoker, but I smoked three cigarettes before giving into the anxiety of my weekend running out and this book not being finished. The anxiety was enough to get me back to the hotel, but the depression was enough to keep me from going back to the room. Going back to the room meant being alone again. So I wandered the lobby, high on speed, drunk on scotch, tweaked out a bit from the overdose of nicotine I just had, and I looked for a girl. I knew I wasn't going to find another *The* Girl in some excited tourist in a Times Square Renaissance hotel lobby, but I wasn't looking for *The* Girl. I just wanted A girl. I just wanted some company. I don't want to die tonight, so maybe I was also looking for someone who would be there to dial 911 just in case. No dice. The lobby was understandably dead. Most people who stay in a hotel in Times Square probably don't spend much time in that hotel. I had one last hope: the hotel bar. One of the first things I found out about this hotel this weekend was that the hotel bar was not cheap enough for me to drink in. But, hey, I've paid for companionship before. I can buy an overpriced drink or two if it means that I don't have to feel this alone in my last dying hours. Surely if anyone was drinking in a Times Square hotel bar on a Sunday they would be as lonely as I am. The bar was fucking dead too. Not only am I alone, I'm alone in my loneliness. I sat down for a drink anyway. The bartender will have to do. I ordered a Johnnie Walker on the rocks. If I'm going to pay top dollar for something, it's going to be something good. I took out my cell phone and set it on the bar honestly thinking that I wanted to make sure I could see it just in case *The* Girl texted.

"I can picture your face well from the bar in my hotel. I wish I'd go to you. I pick up put down the phone like your favorite Heatmiser song goes. It's just like being alone."

Sometimes I don't even have to try to make a song relevant.
No texts.

The bar is closer to the ground floor than the floor that my room is on, so I figured I should probably have another cigarette before I get further away from the only place I can smoke. I walked out, put my headphones in and lit up. Same song over and over. I'm starting to realize that maybe I *am* a bit delusional. I've waited all weekend for *The* Girl to call or text, and even though nothing has come, I still wait...I still hope. But that's just this weekend. I waited years for us to have a chance. And in the time since we got that chance I've waited for her to think, believe, that it was the last chance either of us ever needed.

"Oh God, please don't tell me this has been in vain. I need answers for what all the waiting I've done means. You kill me, you've got some nerve, but can't face your mistakes. I know what I should do, but I just can't turn away."

There was a time when I believed in God pretty strongly. I still believe. I never stopped. But these days you would never hear me characterize that belief as strong. If you knew me—and now that you've read this far you do know me pretty well—you'd probably even find it hard to characterize that belief as existent. But I guarantee you it's there. I was the lead singer of a Christian ska band for five years. I stood in front of these people and sang and talked about how awesome this God was and I convinced people—or at least helped them—to believe it. After five years singing in and handling the band's business side as much as an 18-to-20-year-old kid could, I was kicked out with no explanation. I'm not saying there *weren't* reasons. There were. I'm just saying I wasn't given one. Even if they had given me a reason, I don't think it could've possibly been worse than things some of the other guys had done. Maybe getting kicked out of a band doesn't sound like that traumatic of an experience, but I formed that band in high school with my best and only friends. I was 20 years old when they kicked me out, and it was the first time that I found myself feeling alone since my parents divorced when I was around eight. I felt betrayed by the people I knew as my best friends, and because I firmly believed that God was in control of everything, I felt betrayed by him too. Things haven't been the same since. Technically, I have "turned away" from God. I don't abide by his rules, as you know now all too well, and we haven't been on speaking terms for over a decade. I do, however, still believe. I think that that may be why I'm still here. I always point out the prodigal son story in the Bible. It has to be in there for a reason, right? I'm not that ignorant. I know that, in the story, the prodigal son represents us as sinners before repentance. But I like to think that God understands that sometimes he pushes us so hard that we just need a little break. I'm in my prodigal son phase right now. I've never doubted that someday I'll return. I just hope he takes me back. I just realized—you know, being on the verge of death and all right now—that maybe I should spend a couple minutes thinking about that. Maybe I should stop trolling the hotel lobby and streets of Times Square for any sort of companionship, and maybe I should just go back to my room and find a Gideon's Bible. The thing is— and I've thought about this a lot actually—I was depressed plenty even when I was doing things God's way. Sometimes I think I should go back to church. Maybe I wouldn't feel so fucked-up if I just got back into that. Then I remember how I got hurt by those people just as much as I get hurt by anybody else. Actually, more than a decade has passed since I lost those friends and that trust that I had in God, and I still refer to it as the biggest heartbreak of my life. It had to be pretty traumatic if I can only bring myself to spend one paragraph on it in a book about heartbreak. Someday I hope to write about that part of my life, because I think that it was that experience that put me on the path to where I am now—alone and unhappy, but also ambitious and determined. Delusional? Although, as I've gotten older, I have realized that there were plenty of times back then when I was just as unhappy. There were plenty of times back then when I felt like I was alone. And, you know what, plenty of those times also revolved around *The* Girls. Sorry, God, but I don't think today's the day I'm coming home. I mean, maybe it is in the death sense, but not until I have one more cigarette.

One more cigarette, I swear. I have to finish what I started. I have to get back to that jail cell of a room and do my time. I wish I could say it's because I believe that I'm a writer and I believe that this is what I have to do for myself. Sure, that is part of it, but I'm really doing this for her. I'm doing this for *The* Girl. I'm doing this for a girl who hasn't talked to me in days. If I finish this, maybe she'll see that I really am worth her time. If I finish this and it's good enough, maybe then I'll be good enough for her. I haven't heard from her in days. Is she already gone?

"So go on love, leave while there's still hope for escape. Got to take what you can these days. There's so much ahead, so much regret."

Maybe the last time I heard from her was the last time I'll ever hear from her. Shit. How am I just realizing that now? She said we couldn't get involved. Yeah, her actions said something different, but not recently. Well, sure, three or four days ago, but not now. For months I've been trying to show her that I would do anything to make her happy, to make her feel loved. For months, she's gone back and forth with me—but mostly back.

"I know what you want to say. I know it but can't help feeling differently. I loved you, and I should have said it, but tell me just what has it ever meant?"

I didn't tell *The* Girl #1 that I loved her. Not right away anyway. When I first moved to New York, we reconnected. We went on some dates. We hung out a lot. We had amazing nights together. We slept together a few times, and on more than one occasion, we spent the night together and then the entire next day just lying in bed listening to music and watching movies. I still had my hopes in us, but she didn't. After a lot of time and effort, I realized that she wasn't going to come around. She wasn't ready to receive what I was ready to give. I told her that I loved her and that if she ever found herself ready for me to love her, she should let me know. Only realizing now that I didn't say once she was ready to love me, I said once she was ready for me to love her. Pathetic.

"Are you here because you need someone or because you need me? Forget it, I don't care." I was Lloyd Dobler. I am Lloyd Dobler.

I did tell *The* Girl #2 that I loved her, after she drunkenly said it to me that one night. I think there were other times that we said it, but it was never a common thing.

"But tell me just what has it ever meant?"

I definitely felt like I was falling for *The* Girl #3, but never enough to feel like I should tell her I loved her. Maybe I should've at least told her that I didn't want her to go to France. I'm sure she knew. But maybe I should've said it. Maybe I didn't say it because I knew it wouldn't have mattered. If I had given her a reason to stay, and it wasn't enough, then that would've made the rejection worse. At least this way, I could say she left because she didn't know.

My weekend is almost up. I feel like my life is almost up. Xanax is the answer. It's supposed to quell anxiety, and, holy shit, do I have some anxiety right now. I still haven't heard from *The* Girl. I feel like I am in love with her, but it hasn't crossed my mind to tell her that I love her. Probably because we've never exactly been on stable ground. She scares easily. Maybe I'm getting a little smarter about these things. Maybe my brain isn't as fucked-up as I think it is, and maybe it's kept me from saying it because it's 95% sure that she won't say it back. Yes, there's that 5% that hope hangs on to.

"I can't help it baby. This is who I am. Sorry, but I can't just go turn off how I feel."

I'm not a fucking idiot. I've gone out with plenty of girls and attempted to go out with plenty others who were all very clear about their lack of interest. Some days, *The* Girl makes me think I am a fucking idiot. She makes me feel like I'm wasting my time. She makes me realize that I'm showing her this amazing love that I believe should exist, and she makes me think that I'm showing it to the wrong person. Then, she plans our life out or she tells me what a great date and great kisser I am. There's that 5% that hope hangs on to.

"You kill me. You build me up but just to watch me break. I know what I should do, but I just can't walk away."

The Girl #4 – "Play Crack the Sky" – Brand New

"We sent out the SOS call. It was a quarter past four in the morning when the storm broke our second anchor line."

Nicole and I never even went out on a date—not for lack of trying. I found her attractive from the moment I met her, but she was in a serious relationship (Do I have a type or what?)—and we were friends first, so I liked and respected her enough to not want to fuck with that. I also worked with her, and even though everyone told me after Jaime, "You don't shit where you eat," well, we've established that I am obviously not a person who learns from his mistakes.

For about a year-and-a-half, I never even considered Nicole as anything more than a coworker. At work parties, we'd get into conversations but only because of mutual work friends whom I was closer to.

She didn't believe me when I finally told her I had always found her attractive. At that point, she had lost some weight, experimented with her bangs and really was pretty—to everyone. I almost didn't ever tell her. I figured I'd look like one of the many people who had only just realized it. So why did I wait? Well, I didn't only like Nicole because she was beautiful. I liked Nicole because of her beautiful personality. She was funny without trying to be. She constantly made fun of me for always having headphones in. What she didn't know was that sometimes, when she popped up from her cubicle, I would turn my music off without her noticing just to hear her voice. I was also super attracted to her Staten Island accent. She didn't believe that either. The cubicle in between us blocked our view from each other, but anytime I'd walk back to my desk I'd never miss a chance to get a glimpse of her. I just had to make sure she was really there—that she wasn't just a figment of my imagination. She also made me smile. She seemed to be able to find good in everything. Maybe I hoped that—even though it was nearly impossible for me to do it—she would be the one to find good in me.

"Four months at sea, four months of calm seas to be pounded in the shallows off the tip of Montauk Point."

One thing I did learn from Jaime is that you don't want to be the guy a girl leaves her boyfriend for. I knew that if I was going to have a chance with someone as amazing as Nicole, I didn't want to blow that chance by jumping at it at the wrong time. Then I blew the chance by jumping at it at the wrong time.

In that year-and-a-half that I knew the Nicole with a boyfriend, she constantly tried to hook me up with her friends. I took that as a sign that she saw something in me, and wanted to live vicariously through them. I considered going out with them hoping that they would be exactly like her. I eventually told her that too.

The first friend Nicole introduced me to was a writer, and you know what that does to me. She was smart and funny, and I had a good time with her. We went on one date and then she got a job in London. I don't remember if we even kissed, which probably means that we didn't.

"They call 'em rogues. They travel fast and alone."

153

A year-or-so later, Nicole thought she had the right girl for me: Jess. Jess was pretty, and she loved all the emo and pop-punk bullshit that I grew up on and most people are embarrassed by. She got my sense of humor and had a pretty good one herself. Our first date was spent barhopping around Manhattan until we eventually ended up at a bar called Idle Hands in the East Village—one of my favorite bars in the city, and she bartended there on the side. That night ended well. We kissed and went our separate ways.

The next date was in my neighborhood. She lived in Astoria, Queens, and I lived in Bushwick in Brooklyn. That's not an easy trek. We hit up the crappy bars in my neighborhood and ended up at my place. We fooled around a bit, but she wasn't ready to do anything more. I respected that, and I wanted good reviews getting back to Nicole. The next date, I went to her place. We watched some *Dexter*, ordered Chinese food, fucked, and then we hung out a little longer. I shouldn't remember this as clearly as I do because it makes me look like even more of an asshole. While we were chatting, she said, "Don't tell Nicole I told you this, but she broke up with her boyfriend." Fuck, I thought, Nicole's single? I had to break it off with this girl. But is that what I did? No. I had sex with her again that night before I left. I am an asshole, I know. Jess finally realized that and broke it off with me.

We did, however, decide to stay friends. Then we went to see Reggie and the Full Effect together, had a great time, went back to her place, and had sex again. Does that make me an asshole? I made it pretty clear to Jess that we weren't going to have a relationship, and she was into it as much as I was. We figured we could both just have some good sex and that would be that. I specifically asked her, "Can we not tell Nicole about this until we figure out what's going on?" I didn't want Nicole to think I was still sleeping with her friend. I wasn't. We had one rebound hookup. Wait, is it still a rebound if it's the same person? What's that called? Anyway, Jess agreed that was the smart idea. Then she told Nicole. Maybe it set me back a little, but it was still only a month after Nicole's breakup, so I wasn't making any moves anytime soon.

"One-hundred-foot faces of God's great ocean gone wrong."

I couldn't start that conversation with her because I wasn't supposed to know she was single. I didn't want to seem like the guy who pounces the second she was available. It was like in the movie *Can't Hardly Wait,* when Jennifer Love Hewitt's character shows up to the party and every guy tries to get his shot with her. Nicole was my Amanda Beckett and I was poor, pathetic Preston Meyers. I knew what I wanted to say to her, but it wasn't the right time. The problem was that—like in that movie when Preston is about to move away for college—I was considering moving back to Texas. I thought that if I could be with Nicole I could be happy in New York. She was that dream that led me here. Every day that went by I feared that some other guy was going to make a move and I was going to miss my chance by not even taking one.

"What they call 'love' is a risk, 'cause you'll always get hit out of nowhere by some wave and end up on your own."

We began chatting at work all day every day, and we were getting to know each other. It was just a few days after she had only been single for a month when I first flirted with her. I told her about a first date I went on the night before and how one of the first things I thought was, "wow, this girl looks like Nicole." That was a good thing, I said. I spent all night on that date wishing the girl was Nicole. Then I said, "Since I'm already complementing you, let me get all this out of the way." I told her that I think she's amazing and that I love how positive she is. I told her how pretty she is, and that I've been fighting the urge to tell her since it seemed like everyone had been telling her. "I think they all just feel sorry for me because I just broke up with my boyfriend," she said.

"I was going to pretend I didn't know anything about that," I told her. "But I don't want to lie to you. Jess mentioned it a while back." I tried my best to keep it friendly and to be there for her. I was pretty miserable at my job at this point, and she gave me a reason to look forward to going in to work when I was on the verge of quitting. She gave me a reason to keep believing in that New York romance when I was on the verge of giving up on it.

Valentine's Day came two weeks later, and she went out with a friend to get her first tattoo. I gave her my phone number and told her she should send me a picture once she got it. When she sent the picture, I complimented the tattoo and then told her that that was really just my way of trying to get her phone number. The very first message I received from Nicole on my phone was a picture of her wrist with the word "Love" tattooed on it. On fucking Valentine's Day! Of course I took that as a sign because I'm a fucking idiot.

The chats went on—all day at work, and then texts from home almost every night until one of us fell asleep. I dropped the occasional compliment to make sure I was at least straddling the friend zone fence. She returned some every now and then:

"You're very handsome."
"If I could go back in time, I'd change things."
"I can't look at your face too long because it makes me flustered."

But she also never let me forget that she just wanted to be friends.

"I think our timing is off."

"I value my friendships."

"One day I'll kiss you and just get it out of the way, and then we can be friends."

"Your tongue is a rudder. It steers the whole ship. Sends your words past your lips or keeps them safe behind your teeth."

I wasn't in love with Nicole, but the more I got to know her, the more I fell for her. I wanted to say the right words that showed her that I'd do everything I could to make her feel like the most amazing woman in the world. Even if it wasn't the right time, if it turned out to be the best thing that ever happened to you, then wouldn't that mean that it was the right time? I figured if I was the best thing that ever happened to Nicole, then Jess would be happy for both of us.

After about three weeks of flirting, Nicole and I met up with some friends from work for drinks. Nicole invited Jess, which was fine because we had all moved on. After drinks, the three of us went to karaoke. I did my usual go-tos: "Hey Jealousy" by the Gin Blossoms, "Just Like Heaven" by The Cure, and then Jess and I did a duet of a song I can't recall. Nicole left. She didn't seem upset, and it was already pretty late. As soon as Jess and I went our separate ways, I texted Nicole. I told her I wish she hadn't left because I wanted that night to be about us hanging out together. She confessed that she had been carrying some guilt because she liked me and found me attractive. But we could only be friends. I told her no one was doing anything wrong and I wasn't expecting to be in a relationship with her. Sure, if she wanted a relationship with me I wouldn't have been strong enough to turn it down, but I knew she couldn't be ready yet. I hoped that as time passed, her feelings would become harder to ignore. I would be her friend, but I wasn't going to stop trying to show her that I could be what's best for her.

"But the wrong words will strand you...come off course while you sleep. Sweep your boat out to sea or dashed to bits on the reef."

Two more weeks of friendly conversation and light flirting passed, and I left to Austin for South by Southwest. I go to the fest every year to spend time with my Texas friends, get drunk and watch bands for five days. The morning I flew out, there was an explosion on the east side of Harlem. I knew Nicole lived on the Upper East Side, but I didn't know how far up, and I didn't know exactly where that explosion was. I messaged her to check if she was okay. I told myself I'd ask her out when I got back. A couple days later, at the music festival, some drunken asshole drove through one of the festival barricades as he was trying to get away from cops. He killed two people, injured over 20, and two more died later. Nicole came to mind again—the thoughts of never kissing her, never being able to hold her hand and walk through New York, never sitting on a couch with her head on my lap just watching a movie. Later, I went to a concert where I saw a bartender who looked like her. "There's a bartender at this party, and I saw her and thought, damn she's cute," I texted her. Then I said, "And then I realized she looks EXACTLY like you." I wanted her to know that even while I was taking a break from everything in life, I was not taking a break from trying to make her smile. "Go for the bartender," she said. I didn't want someone who just looked like Nicole. I wanted Nicole. I must've wanted her pretty badly, because any other South by Southwest in the past, I would've gone for the bartender.

My flight back from Texas was as shitty as a flight experience can be—without crashing I suppose. I missed my connection and got stuck in the Charlotte airport for six hours. It could've been horrible, but Nicole was there for me through almost every minute. I told her how nice the Charlotte airport was. I told her about this woman playing all kinds of songs on a grand piano in the food court. I sent her a video so it was like she was there with me. I sent her a picture and I told her that one day I'd take her on a date to the Charlotte airport. She said, "How 'bout this—that's one date I will go on." I immediately planned that date in my head. Then we just bullshitted some more. We never got tired of talking to each other.

It went on like that for another month or so. The topic of dating came up more often, but it never sounded possible. "There were too many things in the way," she said. To me, that just sounded like, "I want to be with you, I just need you to show me how it's going to work." I never tried to convince her with arguments, but I never stopped trying to convince her by being charming and constantly telling her how beautiful and amazing she was.

I finally convinced her to grab a drink with me after work. We left work together and walked a few blocks to Village Tavern in Greenwich Village, had few drinks and talked for hours. I told her all of the things that I've wanted to tell her in person because I didn't know if I'd get another chance. Then Jess showed up after a date she was on. I wanted Nicole to see that Jess and I were friends so maybe she'd feel less guilty.

After we parted ways, Nicole and I were immediately texting each other. She said she thought I'd like her less once we hung out in person. I told her I like her more. I asked what she thought of me now. She said she thinks I'm honest and genuine and she still likes me. Then I said, "Now let's talk about how much you wanted to kiss me at the bar." She played it off. "Did you want to kiss me at the bar?" She asked. I said, "I wanted to kiss you in the elevator at work

159

before we even left." She said she could've kissed me, but then that would make things awkward at work. That was enough for me. She could've kissed me!

"The vessel groans, the ocean pressures its frame. To the port I see the lighthouse through the sleet and the rain."

A couple days later she had a pretty big crisis at work and thought she was going to get fired. I was up until about 2 a.m. on the phone with her when it happened. If she had lived anywhere in Brooklyn instead of on the upper east side of Manhattan, I would've run as fast as I could to hold her in my arms. I hated hearing her cry on the phone and not being close enough to wipe away her tears. Because this was all so serious, I toned down the "us" talk. I was just there for her, and I loved that she wanted me to be, because that's all I really wanted.

When the weekend hit a couple of days later, I took a two-hour train out to Long Island to interview some bands. We texted throughout the entire day. She kept going back to feeling guilty for talking to me and for letting me flirt with her. I kept going back to "you're not leading me on, I'm not expecting anything." She wasn't leading me on. Sure, maybe a mixed signal here and there—but I knew better than to think she was going to fall in love with me any day now. I just didn't know better than to stop hoping for that.

I almost invited her to come with me that weekend. She would've said no. But there she was, sitting in Manhattan texting me all day. It was like she was there with me. I couldn't understand why she wouldn't just be with me through everything. I guess I could understand—she had only been single for three months. I just didn't want to understand. My fucked-up mind couldn't sort it out. To me, it meant she thought I wasn't good enough. All I had to do was convince her that I was good enough—according to my fucked-up mind. A logical mind would've realized that all I had to do was wait. Then it came.

She said we really had to just be friends. This time, it was different. The crisis at work was still weighing on her, and she said that talking to me the way she had been was adding more anxiety. The last thing I wanted to do was scare her away or be something negative in her life. I loved talking to her about nothing. I loved that if something good happened to either of us, we told each other first. I loved that if one was going through something shitty, we would pull each other out of it. At a time when I hated my job and doubted this city, she restored my faith.

"And I wish for one more day to give my love and repay debts. But the morning finds our bodies washed up thirty miles west."

I told her that I would try my best to stop flirting with her. "Besides," she said, "you don't want to be my first relationship after my breakup. Those don't have a very good success rate." Hello, mixed signals! I didn't want to be her rebound. I wanted to be the last relationship she'd want to stay in. I wanted to treat her so well that she'd forget every other relationship she had before. I tried my best to just be her friend. It turns out that when you think someone is as amazing as I thought Nicole was, you just can't try hard enough.

Two days later we kissed. We left work together and just started walking towards our train stops. Different lines, but in the same direction for a few blocks. Well if that ain't a fucking metaphor. We walked past my first train stop because it was a nice night out. I'd catch it at the next one. I can't remember a word of this conversation, but I remember that we detoured through a side street because I wanted to show her one of my favorite streets to walk down, because it's usually empty and I feel like I have it all to myself—a feeling that you rarely experience in Manhattan. I wanted us to have it all to ourselves. All I could think about was holding her hand as we walked down that empty street. So I took her hand, and before I could wonder if it was the right move, she squeezed it. I saw my second train stop approaching from blocks away. Something had to happen before we reached it. There would be no excuse for us to walk to the next one. A block away from the Broadway/Lafeyette stop, I grabbed her, pulled her close, and we kissed. She seemed surprised—in a good way. I will never forget the look on her face afterward. The way her eyes get so wide when she genuinely smiles. Her eyes get SO wide, her eyebrows raise, and she just has the most amazing fucking smile. It was a quick kiss, but there it was. And we had a block to go.

We crossed the street. She was still smiling. I told her I just wanted to get to know her better and see what happens. Yes, I was falling for her, but, if she and I had gone out and I decided that we didn't work, I'm not so stupid that I would just stay with her. Didn't we owe it to ourselves to see? I also told her that I thought that we owed it to ourselves to have a better kiss. She wasn't entirely convinced, but when I put my hands on her coat, I didn't even have to pull her closer to me. It's like she was waiting for me to do that.

My lips touched hers, and they stayed there. My right hand went around her waist and up her back and my left hand landed on her right cheek. She was convinced. For what felt like forever but was probably just like one minute, maybe she forgot about the guilt. I'd like to think that for that minute, maybe she considered "us." I kissed her like I hadn't kissed anyone in a long time. Just like with every compliment I had given her, I wanted that kiss to show her that this guy was fucking crazy about her. I wanted that kiss to show her that I wanted to be the best thing that has ever happened to her. I wanted to convince her that she deserved to be lifted into the fucking sky and I was the guy who would hold her up there forever. She pulled me closer. Cars drove by, people passed us. We heard their conversations. I thought at any second she was going to feel embarrassed or regretful and pull away. I kept thinking that I should pull away. I didn't want her to think that I needed more than she could give. Pull away, man, pull away! But every time that thought crossed my mind, she pulled me closer, she held me tighter. I'd think it again and her mouth would open and our tongues would touch. There were these seconds when we'd stop kissing and our faces were still that close to each other, and then we'd just start again. Our foreheads would touch for a second like we had to think about it, but by the time our lips were hooked together again, our tongues touched again, by the time our hands held tighter against each other's bodies and we deeply breathed each other in again, there was no time for thought. The kiss was perfect. The moment was perfect. She was perfect, and I thought that maybe she was finally starting to feel that I was, and see that we were. When it came to an end, we were still in each other's arms, and that was perfect too. Holding her, having her body that close to mine felt just as amazing as the kiss. When I think back on this kiss, I wonder if it felt so perfect because I considered it to be our real "first" kiss, or because she knew it was the kiss that she just had to get "out of the way, and we can just be friends." To me, it had all the power a first kiss should, but to her, maybe it had all the power a last or only kiss should.

"But this ain't the Dakota, and the water is cold. We won't have to fight for long."

I left her with that smile on her face—the one that made me

fall for her in the first place. That kiss didn't change anything between us, well, not immediately. That night, we went right back to talking like we did every other night. I wanted to beat her to the punch, so I said that "I know that it didn't change anything and I know that we're just friends." She said it was a "memorable kiss." And she said that now that it was out of the way, we should focus on being friends.

"This is the end. The story's old but it goes on and on until we disappear."

The next day, I had an interview with a band after work and she told me she had plans to meet a friend. When my interview got cancelled, I headed to the lower east side where Jess was bartending at Idle Hands again. I updated Nicole in case she wanted to stop by, and, well, because I hoped she'd stop by. Jess asked, "Have you talked to Nicole tonight?" I knew that Jess didn't know that Nicole and I had kissed the night before because Nicole told me not to get drunk and spill my guts to her.

I had spent the last two weeks joking with Jess about asking Nicole out—testing the waters. If Nicole and I being together would hurt Jess's feelings, then, as hard as it would've been, I would've moved past it. Sure, I thought Nicole could be *The* Girl, but I've thought that before and have had to move past it. I didn't want to have to deal with that with Nicole. So, in one of our previous conversations before this night, I asked Jess how'd she feel if I asked Nicole out. "I'm not that much of a selfish asshole to stop people from dating because you and I dated for a big whole month," she said. She did not say, "Yes, that would hurt my feelings, you asshole." Or "No, don't ask her out." Even after Jess and I had those conversations, she had hung out with me and Nicole. On every

164

occasion that I saw Jess, she would tell me about her dating life. So, the coast was clear…right?

"Yeah, I talked to her earlier to invite her here," I told Jess. "Why do you ask?" Jess replied, "Oh, I just wanted to know how her date went." I tried to force a smile, but I'm not that good of an actor. Jess rubbed it in, "She told you she was on a date, right?" I lied and said she did.

It's not Nicole's fault that she lied to me. When we kissed the night before, I told her that I knew she wasn't ready to be with me but I thought she was worth the wait. She told me not to wait. She told me to go on dates and said she wanted to be the friend who hears about those dates. Without missing a beat, I told Nicole, "I don't want to hear about your dates." So, there. It was my fault. That doesn't make it suck any less.

I got drunker. Guts spilled a little. I told Jess I was bummed that Nicole was on a date, and I told her that she had said she was "meeting a friend." I said that Nicole and I had been talking and that we get flirty sometimes. Jess tried to be a friend to me, but she's not a very good actor either. I could tell she wasn't happy about me liking Nicole enough that I could be this hurt by her. I could tell by how happy she looked when she saw that I was this hurt by her.

I left a few minutes later and texted Nicole. I told her it was stupid of me to tell her that I didn't want to hear about her dates. I told her that I do want to be her friend and that she shouldn't have to feel like she has to hide anything from me. I told her she was right and that I don't want to be the first guy she dates after her relationship. But why the hell do these other guys get that chance? "I don't think it's the right time, which doesn't mean I don't think you're handsome and charming." DAMN YOU, WOMAN!

"I do want you in my life," she said.

"I'm sorry I didn't mention the date," she said.

"I feel bad," she said.

"Calm me and let me taste the salt you breathed while you were underneath. I am the one who haunts your dreams of mountains sunk below the sea."

Those were the last nice things she ever texted me. By this time, I was home in bed and drunk. I called her. I didn't want her to feel bad. I saw Nicole as *The* Girl who I just wanted to make happy all of the time. I told her I meant everything I said the night before. She thought that she could never be close to anyone ever again. That's how everyone feels after a bad break up, I said. She listed our obstacles again. "You can't get past Jess?" I asked. If she could never get past the fact that I went on three dates with her friend whom I slept with twice, then that could be tough. She said she hadn't yet, and didn't know how long it would take. Then she said that she does like me, she is attracted to me. She told me that no one has ever talked to her like I do. "And that kiss," she said. "In 29 years, I have never felt like that from a kiss, no one has ever kissed me like that." Like with every conversation we ever had, this one also ended with "we need to be friends."

"I spoke the words but never gave a thought to what they all could mean."

If we said nice things to each other the next day at work, I don't remember them. That night I was going to a concert and she was going to Jess's bar to "meet up with friends." She said the guy from the night before may swing by. I joked about how I wouldn't stop by, that way I wouldn't ruin his chances. I'm sure we knew I didn't want to see that shit. That night, the night after Nicole said, "Don't get drunk and spill your guts to Jess," she got drunk and spilled her guts to Jess. She told her I've been making advances, I've been flirting, and she's been telling me that we needed to just be friends. She told Jess I kissed her. She did not tell Jess that she flirted back, she liked me back, she kissed me back, or that "In 29 years I have never felt like that from a kiss." But I'm the asshole, right?

"I know that this is what you want. A funeral keeps both of us apart. You know that you are not alone. I need you like water in my lungs."

    I guess I understand that she had to be honest with her friend. I don't understand why she wasn't *completely* honest. Jess was my friend too, and now she thought I was just some asshole who was trying to fuck her friend—her words, not mine. I tried to explain to Jess that I would never have pursued Nicole if there hadn't been the obvious connection. I told her that it wasn't just one-sided and that if things were different, Nicole and I might be able to have a great relationship. Obviously, that's not anything a girl you've dated wants to hear—especially two months after sleeping with you and, especially if you're talking about her friend. She let me have it. "Selfish," "asshole," stuff like that. I deserved it. Within minutes of getting cursed out by Jess, I got a text message from Nicole saying there was no way we could be friends. That was the knockout punch. I wanted to be friends with Jess, but I thought Nicole could be *The* Girl. I guess I was wrong...again.

"This is the end."

"I Just Want To Sell Out My Funeral" – The Wonder Years

"I spent my life weighed down by a stone heart, drowning in irony and settling for anything. Somewhere down the line all the wiring went faulty. I'm scared shitless of failure and I'm staring out at where I wanna be."

I just realized why I do this. Not why I love like I love. I'll never understand that. I *think* I love the way I love because I grew up on 80s movies and listen to too much music that has sold me on a product, that no matter what, I will always believe exists. But it's fucking painful. Why put yourself through that? I've hoped and hoped that I would finally understand that. I've chased it, and I've worked my ass off trying to find the answer to that question. I've met plenty of women who probably would've loved me that way, but I convinced myself that it wasn't what I was looking for because it didn't feel the way I thought it should. And the times that it did finally feel that way, like now, with *The* Girl, it seems like I'm the only one who thinks it feels that way. I don't know if I'll ever understand why I approach women and relationships the way that I do. I tell myself that it's because once it pays off, all this other painful bullshit will have been worth it. What if it never pays off? Well, I won't know if it doesn't pay off until I'm dead, right? And, hopefully, when I'm dead, I won't be able to regret how fucking stupid I was when I lived. I guess I'll find out soon, because I feel like I'm fucking dying. I said I want to live, and I do. I mean, the idea of living more life and experiencing more good definitely sounds appealing. But the idea of living more life and experiencing more bad definitely does not sound worth it. If I survive this like I've survived the others, if I survive this physical pain I have tonight, right now, what does that mean? I'll be stronger? What does that mean? If I'm stronger I can handle more? Fuck that. I don't want to handle more.

"I just want to sell out my funeral. I just want to be enough for everyone. I just want to sell out my funeral. Know that I fought until the lights were gone."

Is that why I do *this*? It's been two days since I locked myself in a hotel room with a bottle of scotch, a bottle of Adderall, a bottle of Xanax and a bottle of Ambien. I've been chain smoking for days. I feel like I'm going to die and, somehow, I have this clarity of mind that has made me—for the first time—understand why I do this to myself. It's like when I put my hand in the fan blades as a kid. It's like when I took all those pills and wrote that note on my dry erase board after that fight with my brother. It's like when teenagers cut themselves after their first high school break up, or dealing with the misery of the Army. I just want to feel something else. I want my mind to focus on my speeding heart or my veins that feel like they're going to burst. I want to stop thinking about *The* Girl. I want to have a legitimate reason for my heart to hurt this much, instead of feeling the pain and only being able to blame it on a girl. Two days ago, I was in pain. Two days ago, my heart fucking hurt like hell. That was before the uppers and downers and nicotine and alcohol. Now, two days later, it still hurts. I honestly can't say if it's any better or worse. Does having something else to blame it on make my brain less fucked-up about it? Fuck no. I've never cut myself to take my mind off of emotional pain—most likely because I'm too much of a pussy—but I would imagine that those who have done it probably realize that it doesn't change or fix anything. Maybe it makes you feel better—or maybe just different—for 30 seconds, but then The Shit is still there. When I put my hand in the fan blades when I was a kid, my parents were still divorced after that. My dad still wasn't around. The night I took all those pills after the cocaine and whiskey, I woke up 15 hours later, and The Shit was still there. My brother was still an asshole. When I touched the train. *The* Girl still wasn't there. If I had jumped in front of it, it wouldn't have changed anything. A surprisingly high percentage of people who fall onto the New York City subway tracks actually survive. With my luck, I'd be one of those assholes. No one would feel sorry for me. Everyone would just hate me for fucking up their commute. Maybe I understand the motive I have when I do this to myself, but I sure as hell don't understand why I continue to let myself get here when it has never improved any situation that I've been in.

"I blame the way that I was brought up or the flaws that I was born with or the mistakes that I've made. They're all just fucking excuses."

I feel like I'm going to die any second now, which I think we can all agree is probably the worst feeling someone can have. When I think about love and how I want to love someone and how I want that someone to love me back, I think of it as the best feeling someone could ever have. That's what makes me feel like I finally understand why I do this to myself. I feel like if I can make myself feel the worst possible way a human can feel without dying, maybe that means that, someday, I'll feel the best way a human can feel. Even after all the shit I've been through, I still believe that feeling true love will make me feel the complete opposite of how I feel right now. When I think of *The* Girl, I truly believe I have a chance to feel that.

I'm running out of time in this hotel room, and I'm sick of fucking feeling this way emotionally and physically—but I can't get *The* Girl off my mind. I can't stop thinking of her or *The* Girl before her or *The* Girl before that one and how I was never *The* Guy for any of them. I'm too much of a pussy to cut myself. So, what's it going to be? Do I take more Adderall and just keep going? Do I take some Ambien and just shut it all down? I feel like I have to keep going? I may not wake up tomorrow and then this whole weekend will have been a waste.

I don't want to feel this anymore—not just the heartache but also the fucking physical pain in my heart. It fucking hurts. I can't remember a time when I didn't hurt. I can't remember a time when I wasn't lonely. I'm not saying those times don't exist. I'm just saying that I don't remember them. I left my little town at 18 because I was lonely there and I thought a new place would change that. I left every other place after that for the same reasons—I was hurt and I felt alone. Right now, at this second, I don't only feel that loneliness that seems like enough to kill me, but I also feel the Adderall, the Xanax, the nicotine and the alcohol that, added up, could very likely be enough to kill me. I don't want to die. I've said this. I just want to stop feeling this. I feel like I'm going to die. As hard as it may be to believe, I don't want to. I still hope—like a fucking moron. But I still do. I still hope for *The* Girl.

I haven't talked to her in days and who knows if I ever will again. I talked to *The* Girl #1 again, but it was never the right time for her. I knew from the beginning with *The* Girl #2 that it wasn't the right time, but I put myself through that anyway. I knew from the beginning with *The* Girl #3 that it wasn't the right time, but I put myself through that anyway too. I should've learned my lesson by the time *The* Girl #4 came around, but here I am again, going through the same goddamn shit I always go through. None of those girls killed me. Is this one going to be the one that finally does? It really feels like she's going to be. Heroin doesn't kill people...until it does. There's a great quote *in Love in the Time of Cholera* that says, "There is no greater glory than to die for love." But if/when I die tonight, how will anyone know that it was for love. Maybe *The* Girl will know. Will she feel guilty? I doubt she'd tell anyone. Where's the glory in that? I can't die tonight. I want to die tonight. I feel like I'm going to die tonight, and I just want to stop feeling that. I just want to stop feeling anything, and the only way to do that is to pop some Ambien and knock myself out. One pill didn't do the trick last night like it should have, and with all the extra Adderall running through these veins now, I'm taking two.

"So bury me in the memories of my friends and family. I just need to know that they were proud of me."

Have you ever felt like you were going to die? I don't mean *thought* you were going to die. I don't mean that split second when your car hydroplaned but you skid to safety, because in that moment you don't really think you're going to die. Your brain goes into defense mode and your reflexes maneuver yourself to...life. It's only after the experience when the shock wears off that you actually get to sit back and think you almost died. I was in a car accident once when I was about 18. I was driving through Texas on my way home from visiting my dad in Oklahoma. On the south side of Waco, my lane on the highway merged and I was distracted, so I didn't notice.

The front of my Ford Ranger pickup truck hit the rear tire of an 18-wheeler. That almost sent me into a spin, but then the back of my truck hit the 18-wheeler again. The front of my truck hit it again and sent me sliding across the median of the highway and into on-coming traffic. Somehow, my pickup coasted back into the median before anyone else hit me. What was I distracted by? I was trying to pick a new fucking CD to listen to. Music. Music almost fucking killed me then. Has it been after me all along?

I don't know how, but I managed to walk out of that accident without even a scratch on me. And when I was playing bumper cars with a big rig, the thought that I was going to die never crossed my mind. It was just panic. In fact, I can't think of an example of when you actually get to think you're going to die. I've had someone put a gun to my head, I've had someone shoot at me, and all I thought of then was, "how do I get out of this alive?" Is feeling like you're going to die something exclusive to death row inmates and, I don't know, cancer patients? And now me. I've mixed my cocktail.

"I was just happy to be a contender. I was just aching for anything. And I used to have such steady hands, but now I can't keep 'em from shaking."

The Adderall is speeding up my heartbeat, but I've felt that before. That's where the Xanax comes in. And a couple of sips of my favorite scotch. In fact, I don't know if this is my favorite scotch. I have never been able to afford a Johnnie Walker higher than the black label. And that is definitely my favorite scotch. But for this special occasion I could only get a handle of red label (quantity over quality). That ought to take care of the dry throat, and mixed with the Xanax and Adderall and soon Ambien, it should take care of this whole life thing. The pounding has spread from my chest to my throat, and what seems to now be moving through my blood stream. My hands grip tight and I feel like my veins are going to burst. My heart is speeding up. I feel like I'm going to die any second. Surely, it'll explode any second. That's what happens right? It's not happening. Am I dying? I have to be. This is what dying feels like. I've felt it before, and I slept, but I woke up. That can't happen this time. I don't think it's ever been this bad. Still pumping and pounding, but where is the bursting? Where is the end, goddamnit? I feel like I'm dying. Pour another glass of scotch. I can't leave any of this behind, and I sure as hell can't take it with me. My throat is dry, I guess from the Adderall and all the cigarettes. A fire hose of scotch to drench it down. Why hasn't the Ambien done its job yet? Do I want the pounding to stop? Do I want the feeling that I'm dying to go away? It goes away when I die, right? So drink up and enjoy it. You're feeling a feeling that few people get to spend time in. Do I let my life flash before my eyes? No, my shitty life is what put me here in the first place. Should I tell my family I love them again. No, they've been through enough and it's about to get worse. No more Adderall. No more Xanax. Just more scotch. Man, that stuff really should be enjoyed, but this pounding and sweating, and pacing and shaking. Am I cold? Wasn't I just hot? Okay, now I'm hot again. Then why the fuck am I shaking so much? Just take the Ambien. And then rest. Wash it down with one last drink—maybe *the* last drink. Cheers to *The* Girl and all of *The* Girls before her, and, if I wake up tomorrow, cheers to *The* Girl that comes after her. The best drink I've ever had. I don't know if the pounding has slowed or if the Ambien has just kicked in and I'm not thinking straight anymore. I'm still cold. I'm tired. My life doesn't flash before my eyes. My little sisters do. Their futures flash before my eyes. Is this what dying feels like?

"'Cause I'm sick of seeing ghosts, and I know how it's all gonna end. There's no triumph waiting. There's no sunset to ride off in."

So this is it. Maybe for my life, but definitely for this story. Best case scenario: I wake up tomorrow and go back to my shitty job and sit at my shitty cubicle and do my shitty work. Who the fuck wants to read about that?

TRACK LIST:

Track 1: "23" by Jimmy Eat World, From the Album *Futures* (Interscope, 2004)

Track 2: "Tortures of the Damned" by Bayside from the Album *Bayside* (Victory, 2005)

Track 3: "Settle Down" by The Dangerous Summer from the album *Reach for the Sun* (Hopeless, 2009)

Track 4: "Poison in My Veins" by Bayside from the Album *Sirens and Condolences* (Victory, 2004)

Track 5: "Megan" by Smoking Popes from the album *Destination Failure* (Capitol, 1997)

Track 6: "Another Travelin' Song" by Bright Eyes from the album *I'm Wide Awake, It's Morning* (Saddle Creek, 2005)

Track 7: "What You Know" by Two Door Cinema Club from the album *Tourist History* (Glassnote, 2010)

Track 8: "Good Things" by The Dangerous Summer from the album *Reach for the Sun* (Hopeless, 2009)

Track 9: "Your Heart is an Empty Room" by Death Cab for Cutie from the album *Plans* (Atlantic, 2005)

Track 10: "Sorry About That" by Alkaline Trio from the album *Goddamnit!* (Asian Man, 1998)

Track 11: "Duality" by Bayside from the album *The Walking Wounded* (Victory, 2007)

Track 12: "Never Feel Alone" by The Dangerous Summer from the album *Reach for the Sun* (Hopeless, 2009)

Track 13: "Miserable at Best" by Mayday Parade from the album *A Lesson in Romantics* (Fearless, 2007)

Track 14: "Kill" by Jimmy Eat World from the album *Futures* (Interscope, 2004)

Track 15: "Play Crack the Sky" by Brand New from the album *Deja Entendu* (Triple Crown, Razor & Tie, 2003)

Track 16: "I Just Want To Sell Out My Funeral" by The Wonder Years from the album *The Greatest Generation* (Hopeless, 2011)

ABOUT THE AUTHOR

Mike Henneberger is a Punk. He's what the professional/corporate world might call a content creator—one of many reasons he hates the professional/corporate world. Unfortunately, it took the creation of that phrase to accurately describe him.

He's a storyteller and a music addict who started putting those two things to use as the singer in two bands back in the day, and later as a contributor and editor for The Vent Magazine, an indie zine that he helped his brother create in Kingsville and Corpus Christi, TX. He's an award-winning photographer, an Emmy-winning producer, and a multi-Webby-honored-and-nominated digital and social media manager and strategist, who has contributed to Comedy Central, Rolling Stone, Billboard Magazine, SPIN, Vice, and Music Mayhem Magazine. He's also one of those Army veterans with major depressive disorder and anxiety disorder, but manages to deal with it with the proper mix of therapy, meds, and creating crazy shit. But mostly…he's a punk who likes to tell stories in whatever way those stories are best told.

He lives in Astoria, Queens, the New York neighborhood that finally felt like home, with his amazing wife who is way cooler and way smarter than him, and has been gracious enough to show such a damaged soul the true meaning of love through the ups and downs of mental illness. Thanks to her, there are far more ups. Mike and The Actual Girl, live with their dopeass shih tzu, Porkchop, who is way cooler than both of them combined.

ACKNOWLEDGEMENTS

Special thanks to those who supported and encouraged me through the craziness: muh wiiiiife Megan Bates, AJ Perdomo and The Dangerous Summer, my Big Picture Media fam Dayna, Paul, Gabriella and Becky, Mischa Pearlman, my early editors Susan Swan and Nora Gutierrez-Perez, and of course Jack O'Shea, Ryan Zwiefelhofer, Brett Detar and Josh Fiedler and The Juliana Theory, Matt Brasch, and Brian Swindle and Have Mercy.

And all the thanks in the world to everyone who made this book possible by pledging on the Indiegogo: Aimee Aviles, Alex Martinez, Alexis De Leon, Alison Farinacci, Allen Hoye, Amanda Jackson, Amber Brown, Amelia Theis, Amy Buchanan, Anne-Marie Womack, Anthony Corrado, April Landin, Ashley Vega, Audrey Bell, Aurelia Guzman, Bailey Steinhauser, Baldé Zamora, Becky Kuntscher, Ben Blair, Ben Daggett, Robert Lyman, Bowie Alexander, Brady McNulty, Bralynn Bell, Brandon Weaver, Brian Frank, Brian Gold, Brianna Reed, Brooke Ostrom, Brookesany deGuzman, Carlos Cooper, Carlos Santellanes, Caroline Hall, Carolyn Hamil, Cary Schwartz, Celina Ramirez, Chris Koger, Claudia Pollard, Corttnee Schmidt, Cory Checketts, Cory Deleon, Courtney Collins, Daniel Pena, David Kuti, Sara Pawson, Dennis Makofske, David Gurney, Dominic Mondragon, Drew Price, Eli Lopez, Elizabeth Bruce, Elizabeth Moses, Elizabeth Solis, Eric Budzinski, Erik Macaluso, Ethan Thompson, Felicia Morales, Felicia Ruiz Simpson, Gabriel Alaniz, Gage Stapley, Victoria Garza, Genevieve Hernandez, Rey Ybarra, Heather Cadwallader, Heraclio Gonzalez, Holly Fedorko, Hunter Taylor, Jaime Guerra, James Armistead Shirley IV, Jamie Glisson, Janice Woods, Jason Perri, Jason Sherk, Javier Vasquez, Jay Peloian, Jeff Stevens, Jen Alber, Jenn Lombari, Jenna Meurer, Jennifer Kress, Jennifer Garcia, Jennifer Vaughan, Jeshaun Williams, Jody Kincaid, Joe Hilliard, Joe Martinez, John D. Garcia, John Highlands, John Slattery, Jonathan Munson, Joseph LaCorte, Julie Abate, Justin Hutto, Justin Lentz, Justin Moore, Kathy Rios, Katie Turner, Kayla Shaffer,

Kelly Geyer, Kevin Bates, Kevin Lynch, Kim Roy, Krystal Emery, Kyle Cochran, Kylie Rupard, Lacey Butler, Laina Carrizales, Lance B. Jones, Laura Diane Williams, Laura Suarez, Leah Ortiz, Leigh Cuomo, Leland Fallon, Leslie Ruel, Lexie Gomer, Leyla McCarty, Lisa Marie Hatfield, Lori Garcia, Laura Warshawsky, Luke Byrnes, Mandy Ashcraft, Marcos Cruz, Marcus Boehler, Margaret Morrissey, Matt Sturdivant, Matthew & Tara Bars, Megan Adams, Megan Hohler, Melisa Guerra, Melita Ogden, Menda Eulenfeld, Meredith Schneider, Micah Galindo, Michael Chinen, Michael Claudio, Michael Garcia, Michele Hernandez, Michele Hernandez, Michelle Laurain, Mike Henneberger, Mike Perez, Miranda Fawn, Molly Allison, Molly Hudelson, Monika Sanchez, Morgan Dunaway, Nicole Buergers, Nicole Padreddii, Omar Feliciano, Paige Compton, Patrick Ginnetty, Rafael Carrales II, Ramòn Noël Garcia, Raquel Pickert, Rebecca Bouchard, Regan Arevalos, Rhonda Borys, Riana C Coles, Ricardo Barrera, Rickey F Mapp, Rochell Overn, Rose Damron, Royal F. Schlitt, Rudy Ramos Jr, Ryan Butler, Ryan James, Ryan Michalak, Sally Shrem, Samantha Fischer, Sarah Garcia, Sarah Wagner Stanley, Sarita Elliott, Priscilla Lerma, Scott Andreu, Sean Layton, Sean Osman, Shadrach Michaels, Sharren Bates, Shelly Dotson, Sonia Lopez, Sarah Ramirez, Stephanie Longoria, Stephanie Russell, Stephen DeKoch, Sterling Hunter, Stuart Rector, Suzette Solis, Tami Randel, Tawnee Ledesma, Theresa Carrico, Thomas Bauer, Thomas Seyfors, Tony Jaramillo, Traci Mondragon, Tyler Morris, Vanessa Garza, Veronica Castellano, Virginia Ferguson, William Henneberger, Yeliza Jimenez, Yvette Gonzalez, Zack Wolder, Zulema Cervantes

And those who inspired it: Jimmy Eat World, The Dangerous Summer, The Smoking Popes, Dashboard Confessional, Bright Eyes, Two Door Cinema Club, Death Cab for Cutie, Alkaline Trio, Mayday Parade, Brand New, The Wonder Years, Acceptance, Taylor Swift, Lisa Loeb, Hopeless Records, Fearless Records, Victory Records (R.I.P.), Interscope, Capitol, Glassnote, Atlantic, Asian Man Records, Triple Crown, Razor & Tie.

Join the Berger Media email list for Rock Bottom bonus content and more videos, podcasts, and free chapters of Mike Henneberger's next book (when they're ready).

RockBottomBook.com

Made in the USA
Middletown, DE
15 June 2020